Awakening the Mind,
Lightening the Heart

The Path to Enlightenment Series

THE WAY TO FREEDOM

AWAKENING THE MIND,
LIGHTENING THE HEART

AWAKENING
the MIND,
LIGHTENING
the HEART

— *by* —

His Holiness,
The Dalai Lama of Tibet

GENERAL SERIES EDITOR, JOHN F. AVEDON

EDITOR, DONALD S. LOPEZ, JR.

HarperSanFrancisco
An Imprint of HarperCollins*Publishers*

The emblem of the Library of Tibet is the wind horse (*lung da*), a beautiful steed that brings happiness and good fortune (symbolized by the jewel on its back) wherever it goes. The image of the wind horse is printed on prayer flags in Tibet, which are then affixed to houses and temples, on bridges and at mountain passes throughout the land. The movement of the flag by the wind sets the wind horse in motion, carrying prayers for happiness and good fortune to the ten directions.

AWAKENING THE MIND, LIGHTENING THE HEART. Copyright © 1995 The Library of Tibet, Inc. All rights reserved. Printed in the United States of America. No part of this book may be used or reproduced in any manner whatsoever without written permission, except in the case of brief quotations embodied in critical articles and reviews. For information address HarperCollins Publishers, 10 East 53rd Street, New York, NY 10022.

HarperCollins®, 📖®, and HarperSanFrancisco™ are trademarks of HarperCollins Publishers Inc.

FIRST EDITION

Library of Congress Cataloging-in-Publication Data

Bstan-'dzin-rgya-mtsho, Dalai Lama XIV
Awakening the mind, lightening the heart :
core teachings of Tibetan Buddhism / His Holiness
the Dalai Lama. — 1st ed.
p. cm. — (The path to enlightenment series ; 2)
ISBN 0–06–061688–1
1. Spiritual life—Buddhism.   2. Buddhism—
China—Tibet—Doctrines.   I. Title.   II. Series.

| BQ7935.B774A93 | 1995 |
| 294.3'42—dc20 | 95–11538 |

00   01   02   ❖   RRD(H)   15   14   13   12   11   10

CONTENTS

EDITOR'S

FOREWORD

*The teachings on mind training set forth
here by His Holiness the Dalai Lama are
based on a text composed in the early*

fifteenth century by Hortön Nam-kha Pel, a disciple of
the great scholar and adept Tsong-kha-pa (1357–1419).
This text called *Rays of the Sun* is a commentary on an
earlier poem entitled the *Seven Point Mind Training,*
whose lines are quoted throughout the book. This
poem is reproduced in its entirety at the end of the
book. By the early part of the present century *Rays of
the Sun* had become somewhat rare and obscure. After
the Dalai Lama's senior tutor, Kyabje Ling Rinpoche,
had heard it explained, it became one of his favorite
works because the book combines, in a way that is suc-
cinct and easy to understand and put into daily practice, the qualities of the mind training and stages of the
path traditions of Tibetan Buddhism. Ling Rinpoche
arranged for the Tibetan text to be reprinted and dis-
tributed, and he taught it himself. Subsequently, the

Dalai Lama has taught it on many occasions, at Dharamsala where he lives, in the reestablished monasteries in South India, and at Bodh Gaya, where the Buddha attained enlightenment. Thus its popularity has been much revived.

His Holiness's teachings presented here were translated and edited by the following team: the Venerable Geshe Lobsang Jordhen, a graduate of the Institute of Buddhist Dialectics, Dharamsala, who since 1989 has been religious assistant and personal translator to His Holiness the Dalai Lama; Lobsang Chophel Gangchenpa, who also trained at the Institute of Buddhist Dialectics and has worked as a Buddhist translator first at the Library of Tibetan Works and Archives, Dharamsala, and later, for over a decade, in Australia; and Jeremy Russell, who, with over twelve years' experience working with the Tibetan community in Dharamsala, is editor of *Chö-Yang, the Voice of Tibetan Religion and Culture,* published by the Religious Affairs Department of the Tibetan Government-in-Exile.

INTRODUCTION

*The Buddha offered many different
teachings, corresponding to the different
interests and dispositions of those who came*

to hear him teach. Yet all of his teachings outline methods through which we can purify the mind and achieve the fully awakened state of enlightenment. Among the different sets of instructions, there is a tradition called mind training or thought transformation. This is a special technique devised to develop what we call the awakening mind, the aspiration to achieve enlightenment for the sake of helping others. This technique was transmitted to Tibet by the Indian master Atisha, who taught it to his Tibetan disciples. The first Dalai Lama received the transmission from Hortön Namkha Pel, and from him the transmission came down to my own root guru, the late Kyabje Ling Rinpoche (1903–1983), from whom I received it.

Its techniques embody the essence of the Buddha's teachings: the cultivation of the awakening mind. I rejoice at the opportunity to impact this tradition, as I follow its practice myself. Although I do not claim to have all the qualifications necessary for giving such instructions, I have great admiration and devotion for them. I rejoice that this precious instruction, transmitted from the Buddha, has actually come down to a person like me in this degenerate age when the teachings of the Buddha have almost become extinct. Whether I am giving this teaching or you are listening to or reading it, we are not engaging in an act of competition. We are not doing it for personal gain. If this teaching is given out of a pure wish to help others, there is no danger of our state of mind deteriorating; it can only be improved.

We can achieve enlightenment only through the practice of meditation; without it there is no way we can transform our minds. The whole purpose of reading or listening to Buddhist teachings is to enable us to undertake the practice properly. Therefore, we should try our best to put what we understand into practice. At this juncture we have obtained this precious life as free and fortunate human beings, able to engage in this practice. We should seize the opportunity. Although it is important to take care of our livelihood, we should not be obsessed by that alone. We should also think of our future, for life after death is something we know little about and our fate is unpredictable. If there is a life after death, then it is very important to think about it and prepare for it. At this point, when we have obtained all the conditions necessary for practicing the

Dharma, the teachings of the Buddha, we should concentrate all our efforts on doing so and make our lives meaningful thereby.

We can do this by engaging in a path that results in favorable rebirths in the future and ultimately leads to enlightenment. The ultimate aspiration is toward achieving the fully awakened state of Buddhahood, because even a favorable rebirth in the future is not very secure. Reflecting on the general and specific faults of the entire cycle of existence, this vicious circle of birth and death, will lead us to aspire for liberation from suffering. In addition, we should be concerned, not for ourselves alone, but also for the welfare of all others.

The special technique for transforming the mind is contained in a poem called the "Seven Point Mind Training," which is elaborated on here in a work called *The Rays of the Sun* by Hortön Nam-kha Pel. What we mean by mind, thought, or consciousness is a very complex topic. It is worthwhile analyzing what is meant by consciousness or mind, especially within the context of Buddhist teachings, because according to the Buddha's teachings there is no creator god; all phenomena have arisen in dependence on their own causes and conditions. We have to analyze what those causes are.

Just as the heat of fire is not created by someone else, for it is the nature of fire to be hot, and just as it is the nature of water to be wet, so there is a something called consciousness or mind, on the basis of which we have feelings of pleasure and pain. In general, if we do not know the nature of a particular substance, we will not be able to transform or make use of it. If we do not understand a country's climatic conditions, we will not be able to judge the right time for planting flowers. Similarly, in order to bring about transformation in the mind, it is important first to identify what mind or consciousness is. Then we have to see how the mind is transformed.

Whether or not you accept the existence of something called mind or consciousness, it is clear that everyone experiences pleasure and pain and that everyone seeks happiness and shuns suffering. This happiness that we seek and desire comes about because of the mind. Therefore, we must identify the nature of the mind and the process by which we can train and transform it. In fact, a transformation of the mind can be brought about only by the mind. So we need to examine whether there is a state in which we can be totally free of all the negative aspects of the mind and what the actual process is for reaching such a state of freedom.

Pain, pleasure, and suffering are dependent on their own causes and conditions. Therefore, it is important to identify the negative aspects of the mind, which give rise to suffering, and try to overcome them. Similarly, we can improve the positive aspects of the mind, which bring about happiness.

Mind training means a technique or a process by which we can transform or purify the mind. All the major world religions, especially Buddhism, have techniques for transforming the mind. But here a unique method has been devised to train our wild and deluded minds. The reason the text is called *The Rays of the Sun* is that it outlines a technique through which we can dispel the darkness of ignorance within our minds. This darkness of the mind refers to our misconception of self and our self-centered, selfish attitudes, the negative aspects of the mind. Just as the sun's rays dispel darkness, this instruction dispels the darkness of ignorance.

At the beginning of his work, the author, Hortön Nam-kha Pal, who was a disciple of Tsong-kha-pa, pays homage to him as a sublime master, invoking his compassion. The words *sublime master* refer to Tsong-kha-pa's great qualities, his having abandoned attachment to the temporal pleasures of the world and his achievement of the highest realizations.

In verses following the homage to Tsong-kha-pa, the author makes salutations to the Buddha, the author of the technique for training the mind, to the Buddha of the future, Maitreya, and to the Bodhisattva of Wisdom, Manjushri. The masters of the mind training tradition in Tibet, the Kadam teachers, are also mentioned. The author pays respect to the Buddha by elaborating his qualities, describing how he is the one who, motivated by strong compassion and love for sentient beings, practiced the six perfections and the four factors for ripening the minds of others, with the purpose of releasing them from suffering and leading them to liberation and the fully awakened mind.

Here, reflecting on how a navigator conveys a ship's passengers to their destination, the author notes how the Buddha, piloting the ship of love and the awakening mind, leads sentient beings toward enlightenment. He too was once an ordinary being like ourselves, but due to the force of his compassion, he trained in the path and was able to transform his mind and achieve final enlightenment. It was compassion that motivated him to achieve such a state, it was compassion that perfected his achievement of enlightenment, and it was compassion that induced him to teach others according to their different interests and dispositions.

This is why the awakening mind is the root of all happiness and peace in the entire universe. In the long run it is the foundation for achieving the state of full enlightenment, but even from day to day, the more we are able to develop an altruistic attitude, the happier we will feel and the better the atmosphere we will create around us. On the other hand, if our emotions fluctuate wildly and we are easily subject to hatred and jealousy, from the very start of the day we will not even be able to enjoy our breakfast and our friends will avoid us. So unstable emotions not only disturb our own state of mind, they also disturb the minds of others. Such uneasy feelings cannot be blamed on someone else, for they are the result of one's own state of mind. This is why an altruistic attitude brings a great sense of happiness and peace of mind.

The greater our peace of mind, the more peaceful the atmosphere around us. On the other hand, fear and distrust arise due to a selfish attitude and other negative mental states. A selfish attitude creates fear and insecurity, which in turn create distrust. So even for the people who have no special faith, it is important to have a peaceful mind. When the qualities of the Buddha are discussed, the awakening mind and compassion are always foremost among them.

CHAPTER I

MOTIVE AND

ASPIRATION

As Buddhists, whatever Dharma practices
we do, whether we are saying prayers or
giving or listening to teachings, we should

begin by reciting the verse for taking refuge and generating the awakening mind.

> I take refuge in the Buddha, Dharma, and spiritual
>   community,
> Until I attain the state of enlightenment.
> By the force of generosity and other virtues,
> May I achieve Buddhahood to benefit all sentient
>   beings.

This verse encapsulates the essence of the Buddha's teachings and especially those of Mahayana Buddhism, the Great Vehicle. The first two lines teach about refuge. The last two teach about generating the altruistic awakening mind.

All who take refuge have a feeling of closeness and trust toward the Three Jewels—the Buddha, the Dharma (his teaching), and the Sangha, the spiritual community of monks and nuns. This is the factor that determines whether or not you are a Buddhist. If you take refuge in the Three Jewels, you are a Buddhist; otherwise you are not. One can take refuge at varying levels of profundity, depending on one's intellectual level. The more you understand about the nature of the Three Jewels, the more you will be convinced of their special qualities. Your seeking refuge in them will then be that much more stable and profound.

The way we seek refuge in the Three Jewels varies. One way is to entrust ourselves to the Three Jewels, viewing them as objects superior to us and seeking their protection, refuge, and support. Another way to seek refuge in the Three Jewels is to aim to become a Buddha one day by acquiring their supreme qualities of knowledge and insight. The two ways of taking refuge demonstrate differing levels of courage and determination. Some people seek the support and protection of a superior person in times of danger and hardship and need the backing of that person in order to accomplish whatever they set out to do. Such people are not really capable of doing things for themselves. However, others are more courageous. They might request some initial assistance, but they are determined to help themselves. They exert whatever effort is necessary to fulfill their wishes. They are intent on becoming independent, so they work hard to realize their goals and rid themselves of problems.

In taking refuge, there are also those who are not very courageous. They entrust themselves to the Three Jewels, praying that they may be given protection and refuge. They lack confidence and faith in themselves to ascend to the status of a Buddha. This is the attitude of people seeking only their own liberation from suffering and rebirth. Those seeking the liberation of all beings are much more courageous. They also entrust themselves to the Three Jewels and seek protection and refuge from them, but their primary aim is to achieve the supreme state of Buddhahood for themselves so that they can best serve others. Such people are determined to eliminate all the imprints of disturbing emotions and realize the impeccable qualities of a Buddha. This mode of taking refuge is farsighted.

Because it is clear that seeking refuge can take various forms and can be done on various levels, it is essential to think about the nature of the Buddha, Dharma, and Sangha and their special qualities while reciting the refuge formula.

> By the force of generosity and other virtues,
> May I achieve Buddhahood to benefit all sentient
>   beings.

These two lines express the awakening mind. By cultivating this special aspiration, the individual aims to attain the highest state of enlightenment in the interest of all sentient beings. Starting from taking refuge, in all virtuous actions the practitioner thinks, "I shall engage in these wholesome activities so that sentient beings may be free of every misery and dwell in complete peace."

The practitioner's good deeds are not geared to self-interest. This aspiration is most marvelous, courageous, and expansive. By the power of this thought, the practitioner sows the seeds and lays the foundation for all the wonderful things in this life and the lives beyond. These lines contain the essence and root of the Buddha's teachings. Although the verse is very short, its meaning is vast and profound. While reciting these lines, we should direct all our Dharma practices, such as meditating and giving or listening to teachings, to the benefit of all living beings. We should not pay only superficial attention to the words but instead reflect on what they mean.

Whenever we do any Dharma practice, we begin with this verse for taking refuge and generating the awakening mind. Usually we recite it three times, although there is no rule that we cannot say it more or fewer times than this. The purpose of three repetitions is to be able to reflect on the meaning while we recite it. Through this practice we should be able to effect a transformation of our attitudes, to positively shape our minds. To do this it may be necessary to recite it many times. Depending on your disposition, you might like to recite the two-line refuge formula many times, then recite the formula for generating the awakening mind in the same way. In this way you can concentrate on one thing at a time and make the practice more effective. After reciting the lines about fifteen times, there should be a change in your heart. Sometimes you may be so moved that there are tears in your eyes.

Only after engaging in a proper practice of refuge and generating the awakening mind should you engage in any other practices, such as saying prayers or reciting mantras. The strength of every subsequent practice depends on the quality and strength of your practice of refuge and awakening mind. It is doubtful whether merely reciting prayers without proper motivation is a Buddhist practice. It may be no more useful than playing a tape recorder. Therefore, developing a positive motivation is crucial in this context. The whole emphasis of our spiritual practice should be directed to creating positive and healthy thoughts and actions.

When we prepare a meal, we need to start with the major ingredients like rice, flour, and vegetables. Spices and salt are added later to lend flavor. Similarly, when the major objective of Dharma practice has been fulfilled by creating a positive and healthy mental attitude, other practices, like prayers, visualization, and meditation, also become meaningful.

All religions are meant in principle to help human beings to become better, more refined, and more creative people. While for certain religions the principal practice is to recite prayers and for others it is mainly physical penance, in Buddhism the crucial practice is understood to be transforming and improving the mind. This can be viewed in another way. Compared to physical and verbal activities, mental activity is more subtle and difficult to control. Activities of the body and speech are more obvious and easier to learn and practice. In this context, spiritual pursuits involving the mind are more delicate and harder to achieve.

It is essential for us to understand the real meaning of Buddhism. It is very good that interest in Buddhism is growing, but what is more important is to know what Buddhism really is. Unless we understand the essential value and meaning of the Buddha's teachings, any attempt to preserve, restore, or propagate them is likely to go off on a wrong track. The doctrine and understanding of the Dharma is not something physical. Therefore, unless it is done with a proper understanding, the mere construction of monasteries or recitation of scriptures may not even be a Dharma practice. The point is that Dharma practice takes place in the mind.

It would be a mistake to think that simply changing our clothes, saying prayers, or making prostrations encompasses the entire practice of the Dharma. Let me explain. When we are making prostrations or circumambulating the temple, all kinds of thoughts arise in our mind. When you are bored and the day is very long, going around the temple can be very pleasant. If you find a talkative friend to accompany you, the time just flies. It might make a nice walk, but in a true sense it is not a Dharma practice. There are even occasions when you could apparently be practicing the Dharma, but in reality you are creating negative karma. For instance, a person circumambulating the temple could be devising a plan to deceive someone or plotting revenge against a rival. In his mind he could be saying, "This is how I'll get him, this is what I'll say and this is what I'll do." Similarly, you could be reciting holy mantras while your mind indulges in malicious thoughts. Thus what seems like the physical and verbal practice of the Dharma can prove deceptive.

We say that the main aim of the practice of the Dharma is to train the mind. How do we do that? Think about those occasions when you are so angry with someone that you would do anything to hurt him or her. Now to be a proper Dharma practitioner, you need to think rationally about this. You need to think about the numerous defects of anger and the positive results of generating compassion. You can also reflect that the person who is the object of your anger is just like you in wanting to achieve happiness and get rid of misery. Under such circumstances, how can you justify hurting that person?

You can talk to yourself, saying, "I think of myself as a Buddhist. The moment I open my eyes in the morning, I recite the prayers for taking refuge and developing the awakening mind. I promise to work for all sentient beings, and yet here I am determined to be cruel and unreasonable. How can I call myself a Buddhist? How dare I face the Buddhas when I make a mockery of their path?"

You can completely dissolve your harsh attitude and feelings of anger by thinking in this way. In their place, gentle and kind thoughts can be evoked by reflecting how wrong it is to be so angry with that person and how he or she deserves your kindness and goodwill. In this way you can bring about a true transformation of the heart. This is the Dharma in the true sense of the word. Your previously negative thoughts can be dispelled and replaced by positive and compassionate feelings for that person. We should note this dramatic change. This is a leap of great significance. It is what is really meant by the practice of the Dharma, but it is not a simple matter.

When the mind is influenced by a powerful virtuous thought, no negativity can operate at the same time. If you are motivated by kind and happy thoughts, even seemingly negative actions can bring about positive results. For instance, telling lies is normally negative, but when you do it out of compassion and a rational thought to help someone else, lying can be transformed into something wholesome.

The altruistic thought of the awakening mind stems from the bodhisattva's practice of loving-kindness and compassion. Therefore, on some occasions a bodhisattva is permitted to commit negative physical and verbal actions. Such misdeeds normally give rise to unfavorable results. But depending on the motivation, sometimes these actions can be neutral, and at other times they can become wonderfully meritorious. These are some reasons why we insist that Buddhism is fundamentally concerned with the mind. Our physical and verbal actions assume only a secondary role. Therefore, the quality or purity of any spiritual practice is determined by the individual's intention and motivation.

People are free to have faith in any religion they like. Those who oppose religion do so out of their free will. People choose to follow religion according to their interest and spiritual inclination. There is no way to compel everyone to embrace Buddhism or any other religion. During the Buddha's own life, he could not make all Indians Buddhists. In a world of diverse tastes and dispositions, everyone cannot be a Buddhist. People enjoy the right to believe or not to believe in religion as they wish.

For us the crucial thing is that we chose to follow Buddhism and are willing to take refuge in the Buddha. Under these circumstances, we are obliged to abide by the words of the Buddha. If we Tibetans do not follow the Buddha's teachings but ask the Chinese to do so, it would simply be absurd. They reject Buddhism; why should they follow the teachings of the Buddha? If they tell lies and indulge in other deluded actions, what can we do? If they are overwhelmed by hatred, attachment, and ignorance, they will not be happy and will cause trouble for others. Therefore, it is the task of Buddhists, including Tibetans, to practice the Buddha's teachings. Our practice should be such that the disturbing emotions—hostility, attachment, and ignorance—are eliminated. Our minds should be free of these delusions, and in their place we should develop positive qualities.

As Buddhists we have statues or paintings of the Buddha on the altars in our homes. We go to temples and monasteries and pay homage to the Buddha.

These are all expressions of our respect and faith. But the real test is how much we truly abide by the words of the Buddha. The Buddha is our teacher, guide, and spiritual instructor. Therefore, the actions of our bodies, speech, and minds should accord with his teachings. Even if we cannot comply with them entirely, we should be earnest in our endeavor. From the depth of our hearts we should have a firm determination to act within the parameters of the Buddha's doctrine. We need to ensure that our daily lives conform with our claim to be Buddhists. If we cannot do this, our declaration will be superficial and meaningless. If, under the guise of being Buddhists, we ignore and neglect the words of the Buddha, this is a form of deceit. It is contradictory and deplorable. There should be harmony between what we say and what we do.

When we begin our Dharma practice, we recite the prayers for taking refuge and developing the awakening mind, but at the same time we should create a healthy motivation inspired by kindness and compassion. This kind of practice should be done by both teacher and students alike. When I sit on a throne, I am not supposed to think of how great I am. I also should not think that I am the Dalai Lama and can say whatever I like to those who follow me. Such an attitude would be unbecoming. I am a simple Buddhist monk and a follower of the Buddha. My responsibility is to try my best to implement the teachings. When I practice the teachings, I am not trying to please or flatter the Buddha. The fact of the matter is that I am concerned for my own happiness and suffering. Whether I enjoy happiness or experience misery rests entirely in my own hands. These fundamental factors motivate me to engage in practice of the Dharma.

The Buddha has taught from his own experience what is of benefit in the long run and what is harmful. I, for one, want happiness and hope to avoid suffering. This is an aspiration whose duration goes beyond months, years, or even the whole of this life; it extends to lives without end. In order to achieve happiness and gain freedom from misery in life after life, I have to recognize that the three poisons—the disturbing emotions of desire, hatred, and ignorance—are my enemies. Ignorance—the belief that things exist as they appear, independently and autonomously, without depending on causes—is the root of these delusions. To counteract these ignorant and self-centered thoughts, I need to generate loving-kindness, compassion, altruism, and the wisdom understanding emptiness.

I believe that my destiny lies entirely in my own hands. What the Buddha taught makes great sense in my life. His words are becoming clearer, and what he taught 2,500 years ago is as relevant as ever. Even though I cannot fathom the depth of all his teachings, I can infer his intention in relation to his explanation of the two truths (ultimate truth and conventional truth), the Four Noble Truths (suffering, its origin, its cessation, and the path to its cessation), and so forth. As I listen to and think about the philosophy the Buddha taught so long ago, there is hardly anything that does not make sense to me. I gain great benefit from his teachings, and I believe that others in turn may benefit from my words. It is with this intention to help that I share my ideas and experience. When we are helpful to other people, we are doing a service to the Dharma. Helping even one person is valuable.

The Buddha initially developed the altruistic thought and then engaged in the accumulation of virtue. Finally he attained the enlightened state of Buddhahood. He did so purely in the interest of other sentient beings. Inspired by the awakening mind, which is more concerned for others than oneself, the Buddha perfected his training on the path. Due to his altruism, the Buddha worked to accomplish the well-being of other sentient beings. For eons he was dauntless in that pursuit. Even after attaining enlightenment, it was that force of altruism that led him to turn the wheel of the Dharma. So the underlying theme of Buddhism is to be helpful to others. When we can help others generate virtue in their hearts, make them happy and their lives meaningful, that is a true service to the Buddha and his doctrine. We need to be diligent and direct our best efforts this way. That, I believe, is how to fulfill the other's welfare as well as one's own.

The traditional custom of a teacher's making three prostrations to the throne before taking his or her seat upon it is very important. The purpose is to avert arrogance. When you sit on a high throne and give teachings, people pay their respects by making prostrations to you. Under such circumstances you have to be particularly careful. Otherwise there is a great danger of arrogance creeping in. In some cases this has occurred. Certain monks, who were initially very simple, found they had a lot of students and had attained some status, and they became puffed up. You can't blame them; it was the result of their own disturbing emotions.

The disturbing emotions are extremely cunning and tough. When a person under their sway is seated on the throne, he is ruled by delusion. As we listen to him talking, his pride swells the longer he carries on. This is how the disturbing emotions operate. The effect of the disturbing emotions is amazing. They can make a master quarrel with others out of desire for more students. In such cases, both attachment and animosity are at work.

Fortunately, there is a power that can fight disturbing emotions. It is wisdom. This wisdom becomes clearer and sharper when we apply analysis and examination. It is forceful and enduring. On the other hand, the ignorant mind, although it can be cunning, cannot withstand analysis. Under intelligent examination, it collapses. Understanding this gives us confidence to tackle the problems created by the disturbing emotions. If we study and reflect, we can gain a good understanding of wisdom and the disturbing emotions like hostility and attachment, which are produced by the mind that believes that things are true, that they exist as they appear. The mind conceiving of true existence is extremely active, forceful, and crafty. Its close companion, the self-centered attitude, is equally hardy and willful. For too long we have been thoroughly under its power. It has posed as our friend, support, and protector. Now, if we are careful and judicious, we should develop the wisdom that understands that things do not exist as they appear, that they lack this type of truth; this is called the wisdom of emptiness. By employing this weapon with sustained effort, we will have the chance to fight back against the disturbing emotions.

In the course of our practice we need to think about the advantages of cherishing others and the defects of self-centeredness. In the long run the thought of concern for others will prove superior, and our selfishness will appear in a poor light. It all depends how serious and diligent we are. If we can prove ourselves by pursuing the right path with concerted efforts, we can be certain that the disturbing emotions can be removed.

Buddhahood is the ultimate goal of our practice, and it would be useful to understand what this means. The Tibetan word for *enlightenment* has two parts; the first refers to purification and the second to enrichment or fullness. What we primarily have to purify are the defects of our minds. Such purification does not imply the momentary cessation of these defects. It indicates the deliberate act of applying antidotes and completely eliminating them.

Now the defects we are referring to are the sources of suffering: karma and the disturbing emotions as well as the imprints left by them. These defects can be removed only by applying appropriate antidotes. The imprints left by disturbing emotions obstruct individuals from gaining omniscience. Consciousness, by its very nature, has the potential to know everything, but these defects veil and obstruct the mind from such knowledge. Eliminating these obstructions by developing the necessary opponents is accomplished by the mind. When the consciousness is totally free from obstruction, it automatically becomes fully aware, and that person awakens to full enlightenment.

The state of enlightenment is not some kind of a physical entity like a heavenly abode. It is the intrinsic quality of the mind revealed in its full positive potential. Therefore, in order to reach this state of awakening, the practitioner has to begin by eliminating the negativities of the mind and developing positive qualities one by one. It is the mind that actively applies the antidote in the process of removing the negative impulses and obscurations. There comes a point when the disturbing emotions and mental obstructions can never recur, no matter what happens. By the same token, it is the mind that is exclusively involved in developing spiritual insight and knowledge. However small the positive energy may be to begin with, in due course the mind becomes fully consummated with knowledge and awakens to Buddhahood.

Each of the world religions has its distinguishing features and its own followers. But, essentially, they share a number of common aims and objectives. Consequently, they have been a source of benefit for millions of people throughout the centuries. There is no denying that through sincere practice, followers of religion gain peace of mind and become more disciplined, civilized, and better people. They do themselves good, and many are of great service to humanity. However, many social and political problems also arise from the abuse of religion. People fight those of other faiths, sometimes even to the point of full-scale war. Nevertheless, we should respect the variety of religions because people have different mental dispositions and inclinations, different tastes and interests. One religion, therefore, cannot satisfy everyone. From this point of view, variety is to be admired.

Each religion is useful in its own way. It is futile to imagine there should be one religion for the whole world. It is not as if every Indian embraced Buddhism even during the life of the Buddha himself. This is true of other religions and their founders, too. Therefore, I believe in a harmony of religions, which is practical, applicable, and can produce positive results. I admire the good deeds of those who belong to other faiths. This is a very good way to make friends. I have many good Christian, Muslim, and Hindu friends. In this context, engaging in philosophical disputes and arguments seems meaningless to me. What good does challenging the theoretical positions of other faiths do?

Instead of fostering mutual rivalry and dispute among religious people, I suggest that we learn from other faiths. Tibetan Buddhist monks can follow the example of Christians engaged in social service. Many of them dedicate their lives to the service of the poor, needy, and downtrodden. In Calcutta, there is Mother Teresa, for example. Many Christians care for lepers with a total disregard for their own lives. Is there any Tibetan monk doing that? Nearly a thousand years ago, the great Tibetan master Drom-tön-pa actually did such great work and lost his limbs. More recently, Te-hor Kyor-pön Rinpoche also took care of people suffering from leprosy. Therefore, rather than being confrontational, it would be wiser and more meaningful to learn from each other. In this way, religious people can play a positive role in creating peace and harmony in our world.

Because people are different and their mental inclinations vary, the Buddha taught a variety of philosophical views. The whole purpose of his teaching is to benefit sentient beings, ultimately to lead them to peace and enlightenment. The Buddha's teaching is not a rigid doctrine that requires all adherents to follow one and the same philosophical theory. On the contrary, the Buddha gave various levels of explanation to suit his disciples' varying degrees of intelligence and mental disposition. Consequently, in India, four major schools of thought came about. Even among the four major schools of thought, there are numerous sub-schools.

It is important to remember that all the Buddha taught was meant to help sentient beings and guide them on the spiritual path. His philosophical teachings were not just abstract speculation but part of the processes and techniques for combating disturbing emotions. We can appreciate the appropriateness of the antidotes for different disturbing emotions from our own experience. The Buddha taught that to counter anger and hatred we should meditate on loving-kindness. Paying attention to an object's repulsive side serves to deflect attachment to the object. There is much logical reasoning to show that the appearance of true existence is a mistake. The conception of true existence is an ignorant one, and the wisdom realizing emptiness is its direct opponent.

From such teachings, we can infer that the disturbing emotions are only temporary afflictions of the mind and that they can be completely eradicated. When the mind is free of defilements, the potential of its true nature—clarity and awareness—is fully revealed. As understanding of these is enriched, the practitioner comes to appreciate the possibility of attaining nirvana and Buddhahood. This comes as a wonderful revelation.

We do not have to regard the Buddha's words as something sacred that we cannot investigate. On the contrary, we are free to examine and verify his teachings. The practitioner is able to taste the flavor of the Buddha's teachings by putting them into practice. As a result of personal experience, an individual gains conviction and faith in the teachings. This, I think, is unique to Buddhism. In other religions the word of God or the creator is considered absolute.

There are two major goals of the spiritual path in the Buddhist context. These are higher rebirth and what is known as definite goodness, which refers to liberation from rebirth and reaching complete enlightenment. It is fascinating to listen to an explanation of the detailed methods for achieving these goals. The disciple is not asked to worship the Buddha in order to attain higher rebirth. It is explained that higher rebirth can be achieved by the ethical practice of abandoning unwholesome actions. Such an instruction is realistic and logically sound. Therefore, an individual who wants to attain higher rebirth, such as birth as a human being, must avoid unwholesome deeds.

Now to be reborn as a prosperous, good-looking person who enjoys a long life, there are further sound instructions. To become wealthy in the future, we need to practice generosity in this life. If you want to be handsome with an attractive personality, you are advised to practice patience and tolerance. In order to enjoy a long life, you are instructed not to harm other living beings but to do what you can to help them. These causes and consequences are logically tied together.

With due respect to other religions, I believe that only Buddhism instructs its followers to develop faith and conviction on the basis of logic and reasoning. There is absolutely no coercion or compulsion to believe. In fact, a rational approach is highly respected. The Buddha has said that an individual attains a higher rebirth by creating positive actions and abandoning negative actions like killing, stealing, and so forth, not just by offering a thousand butter lamps to the Buddha. It is not just faith that gives rise to wonderful results, but paying attention to the right causes.

Let us examine one particular instance. The Buddha has instructed us to practice patience so that we will be reborn as beautiful people. The indications are obvious. When a person is angry, his red eyes bulge and his face is disgusting, whether or not he usually has a nice face. Nobody wants to be around someone who is angry, whereas when someone smiles, we are attracted, even if it is a stranger.

The fundamentals of the Buddha's teaching concern observing the law of cause and effect and practicing the Four Noble Truths. Therefore, those who desire happiness, prosperity, and ultimately liberation need to adhere to these fundamentals. If we want positive results, we must attend to their proper causes. This can be simply illustrated as follows. When we want to improve our financial circumstances, it would be stupid to hold onto our capital and hide it under our belts. It will not increase by itself; we have to invest it. This means that initially we have to part with our money. We can, therefore, understand the Buddha's logic when he says that it is important to practice generosity if we want to become wealthy in future lives. From examples like this, we can infer that we can trust the words of the Buddha. What he taught out of his own experience and knowledge is relevant and useful for each of us.

CHAPTER 2

SOURCE AND QUALITIES

OF THE INSTRUCTION

What the Buddha has taught to make our
lives meaningful and happy is wonderful.
We all share common desires to be happy

and not to be miserable. But how people go about fulfilling these aims can be very different. It largely depends on the individual's mode of thinking. This in turn depends on the kind of instruction he or she has received as well as the person's cultural background. The Buddha's teachings discuss many ways of engendering compassion, patience, an understanding of reality, and so forth. The teachings include many impressive arguments that can help us discard negative states like hostility and violence. The Tibetan cultural heritage has been greatly enriched by the Buddha's teachings. Consequently, our people enjoy great peace of mind. With the invasion of Tibet by the Chinese, many Tibetans have become refugees. Obviously, the life of a refugee is fraught with difficulties. I have met refugees from other parts of the world and found their attitude to be very different from that of the Tibetans. They are beset with anxiety and worries. By contrast, some Tibetans have told me that they were even able to do their spiritual practice while they were in the Chinese prison and that their time there was peaceful and fruitful.

It is essential that we preserve and promote the Buddha's teaching, which, as a source of peace in the world, is of benefit to all sentient beings. Although every Buddhist should take interest in this, ordained monks and nuns have a special responsibility. Starting with myself, we ordained people must act scrupulously according to the monastic discipline. The vows of ordination should not be taken lightly. Anyone considering them should think very carefully beforehand and should have a strong sense of renunciation. Becoming a monk or nun does not mean entering an easygoing life of indulgence. On the contrary, a candidate for ordination should see the Buddha, who underwent many hardships in his spiritual quest, as a model. Some people may have the impression that merely holding certain ritual implements is all that is required to gain spiritual insight. They are clearly unaware of the sacrifice and effort involved in gaining actual insight.

In Buddhism, quality, not quantity, is what really counts. The Dharma is not preserved or propagated by force. So a greater or lesser number of monks and nuns makes little difference on that score. However, if the ordained people are unruly or misbehave, it harms the Dharma. I therefore insist on quality and have often stated that there is no use in simply having many monks and nuns. Some people object, but I have sound reasons for what I have said. The true value of Dharma can be revealed by ten good practitioners. Even one highly qualified practitioner can make the virtues of Buddhism shine.

There is great merit in taking ordination as a monk or nun if you do so in a proper manner and with the right motivation. Therefore, before deciding to do so, you should examine and confirm your intention. You should be aware of the benefits and purpose of what you are doing. Change should begin with mental transformation. Mere physical change does not achieve the whole purpose. Those who lack a commitment to mental transformation and misbehave set a bad example and cause the people's faith to decline. So when I talk about quality, I am referring to people gaining a proper understanding of the Dharma and putting those teachings into practice in their daily lives.

These days, there is some religious freedom in Tibet. People are allowed to become monks and nuns and to rebuild some of the monasteries destroyed by the Chinese. Some Tibetans who have lately visited Tibet have told me that the monks and nuns there have not had a proper religious education and only engage in performing ritual. Others have had the impression that the monks and nuns in Tibet are really religious minded and dedicated to the pursuit of spiritual practice. Rebuilding the sacred Buddha Dharma must be done with the utmost care and attention.

The text I am reading from, *The Rays of the Sun,* opens with the following verses:

> Arising from the source of love and compassion
> The ship of the awakening mind is well launched.
> Above it billow the great sails of the six perfections
>   and the four ways of amassing disciples,
> Which are driven by the wind of enthusiastic
>   effort that never slackens.
> Perfectly it carries embodied beings across the
>   ocean of the cycle of existence
> Landing them on the wish-fulfilling jewel island
>   of omniscience.
> I prostrate, placing my head at the feet of the
>   leaders of the spiritual lineage:
> The Subduer who is our supreme navigator, the
>   powerful [Buddha];
> Maitreya and [his followers] Asanga, Vasubandhu,
>   and Vidyakokila;
> Manjushri and [his followers] Nagarjuna and the
>   supreme wise saint Shantideva;
> The master of the Golden Isle [of Sumatra] and
>   [his disciple] the noble Atisha;
> And [his Tibetan disciple] Drom-tön-pa and his
>   three spiritual brothers [Po-to-wa, Phu-chung-
>   wa, and Chen-nga-wa].

In these lines homage is paid first to the Buddha Shakyamuni as the supreme navigator who expounded the perfect path based on his own experience of the awakening mind and the six perfections (generosity, discipline, patience, effort, concentration, and wisdom). The lineage of far-reaching altruistic activities was passed from Maitreya to Asanga to Vasubandhu and down to his followers. The lineage of profound insight was passed via Manjushri to Nagarjuna and then to Shantideva. The great Indian master Atisha became like a confluence of both these traditions, and what is known as the lineage of the blessings of the practice was passed from him to Drom-tön-pa and the subsequent followers of the Kadampa tradition—the twelfth- and thirteenth century Tibetan practitioners following Atisha noted for the purity and the unpretentiousness of their practice. The author pays great respect to them all.

> I prostrate at the feet of the great emanation of
>   Manjushri, Tsong-kha-pa, the second
>   conqueror of these degenerate times,
> Who propounded the individual spiritual paths
> Of these great pioneers with extreme lucidity and
>   coherence.

The author was a direct disciple of the great Tsong-kha-pa and pays special homage to him by recounting some of his preeminent qualities. Tsong-kha-pa is venerated as among the greatest of Tibet's saintly scholars. He had fathomless knowledge of both sutras and tantras. His collection of writings testifies to his scholarly credentials; he wrote eighteen volumes altogether.

In writing his own treatises, he studied numerous classical Indian texts thoroughly and did exhaustive research to ascertain their intention. When we study his works, we can really appreciate his scholarly acumen and precision. He was especially distinguished for discussing the more difficult and finer points of philosophy, which was rare among the great scholars in Tibet. Bu-tön, a renowned scholar of the previous generation, wrote very extensively, in fact more than Tsong-kha-pa, but he did not deal with philosophical points as thoroughly. Because of this, there is a saying among the scholars of Amdo, northeastern Tibet, "If you need references, consult Bu-tön, but if you have philosophical doubts, consult Tsong-kha-pa."

When we study the works of different writers, we get some feeling for their personalities. Some go into great detail but are not very clear and precise when it comes to stating theoretical positions. Others are more concise and straightforward when it comes to theories and philosophical tenets. Writers reveal their own personalities in their writing. They are like the human face. Even though everyone has the same number of features within the small area of the face—two eyes, one nose and so on—still no two faces are identical. There are as many different faces as there are people.

> Supreme among his wonderful teachings
> Are the means for activating the awakening mind.
> I shall expound his perfect teaching with absolute
>   accuracy;

Those fortunate to follow the way of the Great
Vehicle should pay close attention for true
appreciation.

There is a fine tradition according to which writers
begin their work by stating their commitment to compose. This serves as an encouraging stimulus to complete their project. Our author here says that he is
going to compose his text according to the instructions
of his master. Tsong-kha-pa wrote nothing exclusively
concerned with mind-training teachings. His disciple,
Nam-kha Pel, wrote this text as a supplement to
Tsong-kha-pa's works.

This mind training is called an ear-whispered transmission because its teachings are passed orally from
teacher to student. First it gives a historical account of
the tradition and then discusses the meaning of the actual text. To demonstrate the greatness of this instruction, the historical account quotes the "Seven Point
Mind Training," the poem by Geshe Che-ka-wa that I
explain in this book.

The essence of this nectar of secret instruction is
transmitted from the master from Sumatra.

All of the extensive teachings given by Buddha
Shakyamuni, the collection of 84,000 teachings, are
meant for removing our mistaken attitude, the misconception of self, and for training our minds to benefit others. All these teachings are meant for removing

the collection of 84,000 disturbing emotions, as well as birth, sickness, old age, death, and the other sufferings generated by them. Such instructions are referred to as nectar. The Sanskrit term for nectar means "that which grants immortality." A skilled physician who knows how to administer such nectar properly can relieve a patient from sickness and even death. Similarly, through following such instructions as these, we can be liberated from such problems as death, old age, and so forth.

The practice of the awakening mind is like just such an elixir. If you practice in the tradition of those intent on personal liberation, of course you can attain freedom from death, old age, birth, sickness, and even the cycle of existence. But it is only by generating the awakening mind, supplemented by other practices, that you will be able to attain the state of Buddhahood. Therefore this practice of mind training, which is a means to generate the awakening mind, is actually the essential practice. This instruction is called the essence of the nectar because by following it you can achieve the state of immortality, which is actually liberation. There are two methods explained in the Buddha's teachings: the method that leads to achieving personal liberation and the method that leads to the fully awakened state of a Buddha. All these traditions were held by the great teacher from Sumatra, known as Ser-ling-pa. Atisha (982–1054 C.E.) received his training in the awakening mind especially from Ser-ling-pa.

Atisha, the great Indian master, had countless disciples in India, Kashmir, Nepal, and Tibet, but of these the greatest was Drom-tön-pa (1005–1064). He was the real holder of the lineage of Atisha. He was a great practitioner, who even to ordinary perception had achieved the awakening mind. It is due to his kindness and hard work that the Kadampa tradition came into being in Tibet. Drom-tön-pa in turn had many outstanding disciples, but there were three main ones, Po-to-wa, Chen-nga-wa, and Phu-chung-wa, known as the three Kadampa brothers. Chief among these was the great spiritual master Po-to-wa (1031–1106), who inherited the mind training lineage. Po-to-wa was extremely successful in developing the Buddhist doctrine and focused primarily on the thorough practice of the six principal texts of the Kadampas.

Po-to-wa's main practice was generating the awakening mind. He had more than two thousand disciples from all regions of Tibet determined to attain liberation. Two from central Tibet were compared to the sun and the moon, the great Lang-ri Tang-pa Dorje Seng-ge (1054–1123) and Sha-ra-wa Yön-den Drak (1070–1141). Sha-ra-wa possessed the complete instruction and transmitted his lineage to more than 2,800 monks. Of his four principal disciples who were responsible for passing on his lineage, Che-ka-wa was responsible for the teachings on mind training and generating the awakening mind.

Che-ka-wa once heard the "Eight Verses for Training the Mind" by Lang-ri Tang-pa, which caused him to develop a strong interest in this teaching. He visited Lhasa in search of more teachings on mind training. Some of his wise friends told him that because a spiritual master of the Great Vehicle tradition should be worthy of esteem, he should seek out either the great Sha-ra-wa or Ja-yul-wa. Accordingly, he visited Sha-ra-wa, who was staying at the House of Sho in Lhasa. When Che-ka-wa arrived, Sha-ra-wa was giving a teaching on the levels of those who aspire for liberation. At first Che-ka-wa was not very impressed, because he did not find what he was seeking. The mind training practice of exchanging oneself with others in order to develop altruism was not even mentioned. Afterward, he felt confused and began to wonder whether such a practice of mind training still existed and whether this master possessed the lineage.

The next day, while the monks were making their alms round, Che-ka-wa found the great master circumambulating a stupa. He immediately spread out a mat and asked him respectfully to sit down, saying, "I would like to discuss with you certain things about which I am unclear."

Sha-ra-wa replied, "Since you are a great teacher yourself, what is it that is still unclear to you? I explained everything very clearly when I was seated on the religious throne."

Che-ka-wa then recited the "Eight Verses for Training the Mind" and said, "There are practices here that are useful when, because of my untamed mind, I sometimes face problems like not finding a place to stay or being harassed by others. If I do this practice of mind training, giving the benefit to other people and accepting defeat for myself, I find it very useful. Sometimes, of course, it is extremely difficult to put such mind training into practice, so what I want to ask you is, is mind training appropriate to practice, and can it become a cause for attaining Buddhahood?"

Then Geshe Sha-ra-wa, who was actually turning the beads of his rosary, said, "There is no doubt about the usefulness of the practice of mind training. Of course, whether it is suitable for you or not is a different matter. If you do not desire Buddhahood, that is one thing, but if you really wish to attain enlightenment, then this practice of mind training is essential."

So his actual answer was, "Whether you like it or not, if you really desire Buddhahood, then mind training is the only way." Che-ka-wa thought that since his reply was so forthright, Sha-ra-wa must have great personal experience of the teaching. Next he asked, "Since this mind training instruction is an authentic teaching there should be scriptural references for it. Can you tell me what the source is?"

Sha-ra-wa replied, "Who would not regard it as derived from the work of the exalted Nagarjuna? The authentic source of this teaching is to be found in his *Precious Garland,* where it says, 'May their unwholesome deeds bear fruit for me. May all my virtue bear fruit for others.'"

Che-ka-wa responded, "I like this teaching. Kindly give it to me."

Sha-ra-wa advised, "The practice of this instruction requires constant effort over a long period of time, but if you are prepared to make such an effort, you can take these teachings from me."

Che-ka-wa then inquired, "If this practice is imperative for attaining Buddhahood, why didn't you refer to it earlier when you were teaching? Why did you make no reference to mind training then?"

Sha-ra-wa responded, "What's the use of giving a great teaching like mind training if no one really wishes to practice it?"

I think we need to pay more attention and respect to this ancient tradition of not teaching the Dharma to anyone and everyone without discrimination. In the past, teachers did not teach just anyone who came to them, nor did they give just any teaching that was requested from them. They sought to ensure that appropriate teachings were imparted to appropriate disciples. In that way, only truly dedicated and spiritually oriented disciples became involved in the Dharma, and as a result their practice was very successful. Teaching tantra was severely restricted, and only the most capable and devoted disciples were permitted to receive it. In recent times, such restrictions have been waived, and even tantra has become the subject of popular public teachings.

After making three prostrations, Che-ka-wa went back to where he was staying and, opening a copy of Nagarjuna's *Precious Garland,* found the quotation that Sha-ra-wa had recited. Then, setting aside all negative thoughts, he spent more than two years at the place called Sho putting these teachings on mind training into practice. Then he spent six years at a place called Gye-gong and another four at a place called Shar-wa. Altogether, Che-ka-wa spent fourteen years engaged in developing the awakening mind under his teacher's guidance. Che-ka-wa gained a perfect realization of the awakening mind through emphasizing the exchange of oneself with others. Later he said, "All the sacrifices I have made and the hardships I have undergone have now borne results."

For great beings such as these, spiritual knowledge was not confined to mere intellectual understanding. They were more concerned with spiritual realization than anything else. Neither teacher nor student was under any of the pressure that is so common these days. Consequently, they followed what we might call an experiential method. In this process, students would progress according to their experience of what they had already been taught. A text would not be taught from beginning to end without a break but gradually, in stages. Students would be taught the next part only when they had gained sufficient confidence and experience of the preceding section.

The Kagyu school still teaches Mahamudra, the Great Seal, in this fashion. Dzogchen, the Great Completion, is also taught in this way. But, in general, people these days are in such a hurry that it is common for the entire presentation of the stages of the path to enlightenment to be taught in a very short time. This method of teaching is not so effective in itself, and students do not pay the same degree of attention and respect. They just listen to the teaching as if it were some kind of a story.

Among all the classical Indian treatises, Shantideva's *Guide to the Bodhisattva's Way of Life* is the most authoritative when it comes to the mind training teaching of equalizing and exchanging self with others. Our author here has taken this text as the foundation and inspiration of his own writing. With the statement, "I shall present the instruction according to the tradition of Tsong-kha-pa," our author concludes his account of the source and great qualities of this instruction. The text says:

> You should understand the significance of this
>   instruction
> As like a diamond, the sun, and a medicinal tree.
> This time of the five degenerations will then be
>   transformed
> Into the path to the fully awakened state.

A precious diamond removes poverty and grants all your wishes; even a fragment of diamond is regarded as an excellent ornament, surpassing even the best golden jewels. Similarly, even if you implement only a part of the practice of generating the awakening mind, such as the practices of compassion or tolerance, it will still outshine all other practices. Even the practice of one such factor will bring about a special effect within the practitioner. A bodhisattva, one who champions the awakening mind, may not be actively engaged in the practice of wisdom and the realization of emptiness, but because of his or her realization of the awakening mind, that person will still outshine those embarked on personal liberation only and will maintain the name of bodhisattva. She or he will be able to work for the welfare of other sentient beings. Even if you simply generate the aspiration to the awakening mind and are unable to put it directly into practice, you will still exceed other practices, like those of beings seeking only personal liberation. Through such practices you will be able to remove the poverty of the cycle of existence.

The awakening mind is also compared to the sun because when the sun has risen, not only is darkness unable to obscure it, but even a single ray of sunlight can dispel darkness. So even if you are only able to gain a partial realization by listening to this instruction, you will be able to suppress the self-centered attitude, which is induced by the misconception of self.

It is important to analyze whether our self-centered attitude arises from the misconception of self. Generally, the stronger our misconception of self, the more tenacious our self-centeredness. For ordinary people like us, these two types of attitude are almost inseparable and reinforce each other. Some beings have eliminated ignorance, the misconception of self, but are not as courageous as bodhisattvas in working for the welfare of others. Although their realization of emptiness has dispelled their ignorance, due to their lack of courage and willingness to sacrifice themselves for the welfare of others, that realization is unable to dispel their self-centered attitude. Conversely, bodhisattvas who have not yet realized emptiness can reduce the grip of the self-centered attitude because, due to the force of their awakening mind, they have developed the courage to sacrifice themselves for the welfare of others.

When Buddha Shakyamuni actually appeared in this world the time was already being described as degenerate. Now the times have degenerated even further. Sentient beings are preoccupied by disturbing emotions and continually engage in negative activities. They do not like to see excellence in anyone but themselves, and when they do see someone successful they are jealous and their hearts are uneasy. They become bent on harming other sentient beings physically, verbally, and mentally. At times like these, even the powerful guardians of Buddhism, the Dharma protectors, those powerful celestial beings pledged to protect the Buddha's teachings, can do nothing to help and leave for different realms. Meanwhile, negative spirits multiply and become stronger. As a result, we encounter many inauspicious experiences, especially those of us who profess to have entered into the teachings of the Buddha but who always engage in negative activities. In such a degenerating era, if you do not engage in a practice like mind training to really transform your mind, there will be no other way to continue your practice of the doctrine.

These mind training teachings are a tremendous source of inspiration. The instructions on how to transform adverse circumstances into favorable ones are unique and powerful. Human happiness is primarily determined by our mode of thinking. We Tibetans, for instance, lost our nation and became refugees. The destruction, torture, and humiliation entailed by life under the Chinese is unspeakable. In my own case, I have spent the best part of my life in exile. Because of my karmic connection with the Tibetan people, they have much faith in me, and from my side I try to be helpful to them. But the situation at present is very unfortunate. I cannot help my people directly.

When we Tibetans first came into exile, the only things we were familiar with were the earth and the sky. Our problems were enormous. We suffered from acute financial difficulties, and we did not have enough people equipped with modern education. And as if those hardships were not enough, we were in conflict with the People's Republic of China—an enormous power. That is why I sometimes joke with people that if the Dalai Lama did not have some understanding of the Dharma to fall back on, he would be taking sleeping pills by now. But I do fine without them. Even though I do not have any spiritual realization, some understanding of the teachings greatly helps in times of despair. The Buddha taught that as long as you conceive of true existence and as long as you are dominated by self-centeredness, you will have no peace or happiness. These fundamental teachings help you relax when things go wrong and equip you to face hard times. The oppression and persecution the Tibetans have suffered and continue to suffer under Chinese rule is one of the greatest human tragedies. But just being negative about the situation is not constructive, and losing heart does not help us solve problems. So, in the light of the Buddha's teachings, we should develop courage.

The Buddha has taught that all sentient beings have been kind to us at some time during our past lives. Even our enemies give us the best training in patience. When we reflect on these holy instructions, in a way we should feel grateful to the Chinese. If we were still living in the same old system, I very much doubt that the Dalai Lama could have become so closely acquainted with worldly reality. I used to live in a very sheltered environment, but now that we are in exile, there is no stigma attached to facing reality. In our own country, we could pretend that everything was in order because it was shrouded under a cloak of pomp and show. I had to sit on a high throne assuming the attitude of being the Dalai Lama. Some of the older officials will recall that in Lhasa our government officials were more concerned about elaborate functions and their rich clothes than the nation's welfare. They felt they could afford to pretend that everything was fine even when disaster was looming on the horizon. It is quite possible that I could have become narrow-minded, but because of the Chinese threats and humiliations, I have become a real person. So what happened in Tibet can be seen as a blessing in disguise.

Our contact with the outside world is another positive effect. If it were not for the Chinese invasion, we might still be sunk in our old system. The old Tibet was very conservative, and there was hardly any room for new developments and reforms. But the rapidly changing world has had some influence. Now our religion and culture are recognized as part of the world's valued heritage. Tibetans have become known around the world and have gained some recognition.

I, too, have had good contact with many people of other faiths. Through exchanging ideas I have gained many friends around the world. Such contacts provide moral support so we no longer feel lonely. After I received the Nobel Peace Prize, people refer to me as a promoter or champion of world peace. At times it is embarrassing; I have done nothing for world peace. I try to generate compassion and meditate on equalizing and exchanging self with others. These practices are for my spiritual development. Thinking about and meditating on nonviolence is also part of my spiritual practice. So what have I done for world peace? I received the title of Nobel Laureate and some money without having to do anything for it.

One thing that is certain is that these mind training teachings have greatly benefited me. When I meet different people and exchange ideas, my understanding of them becomes more obvious. The practice of developing a kind heart and an altruistic attitude gives great inspiration and helps us relax and broaden our perspective in times of despair. We must see the mind training teachings in this light. The instruction to transform adversity into a favorable situation is exceptionally valuable.

In this age of degeneration, sentient beings cannot bear their own sufferings and rejoice when their enemies are afflicted. However, putting into practice this instruction for transforming adversity into favorable conditions for achieving enlightenment will be very powerful and effective. In our modern world there has been great material development and far-reaching intellectual achievement, but anxiety remains. Generally, when we meet with adverse circumstances, they cause us to lose our tempers, our powers of judgment fail, and we become discouraged and depressed. But for a practitioner of mind training, these adverse circumstances provide favorable conditions, just as poison can sometimes be transformed into something beneficial like medicine. When the very circumstances that cause ordinary persons to create disturbing emotions can be transformed into favorable conditions, it is really marvelous. A practitioner who can do this is called a person of great intelligence, a person of great capacity.

Although I do not claim any high realization in the practice of mind training, I have sincere admiration for and faith in this instruction. So when I hear things being said against me and when I meet with adverse circumstances, I try to apply the instructions outlined here. A practitioner who can transform adverse circumstances into favorable conditions will be affected by nothing. Whether that person is traveling or staying in one place, eating or doing anything else, he or she will be constantly aware of working for other sentient beings. Deep down, such a person is calm and free of anxiety. The body becomes a realm of joy, because no external circumstances can disturb that person's presence of mind. The body could also be called a conflict-free zone, because for that person, there is no inner conflict and no external circumstances can upset him or her.

Adverse circumstances can actually serve as a stimulus of progress in our practice. What is being taught here is a method to decrease the grip of self-centeredness and increase the wish to ensure the welfare of others. Even in this world we see that kindheartedness, an altruistic attitude, is the root for securing peace in the world, whereas a harmful selfish attitude is the source of conflict and unhappiness. So, regardless of the question of life after death, even within this life the mind training instructions yield great benefits. Of course, an altruistic attitude should be reinforced by wisdom. This union of wisdom and compassion is very important. Altruism by itself is not very powerful. So the altruistic attitude that is the target of this instruction is reinforced by wisdom, which is something truly marvelous.

CHAPTER 3

THE MEDITATION

SESSION

*The reason we need to acquire
understanding of the Dharma and put
it into practice is very simple. Everyone*

wants to have happiness and to avoid misery. Happiness and misery arise primarily due to our way of thinking. Of course, external factors and material resources also play a role. But because the mind is the source of happiness and suffering, Buddhist teachings include exhaustive means and methods for transforming our thoughts. If we train our minds to be virtuous and positive, our conduct will automatically become more pleasant and wholesome.

However, many of us know from experience that generating a wholesome mental attitude is not a simple task. It is like rolling a boulder up the hill or pushing a car that has run out of fuel. On the other hand, negativities arise spontaneously and as easily as water flowing downhill. What this makes clear is that we have to make a deliberate effort to cultivate positive thoughts and avoid negative ones.

This is the context in which the Buddha taught the Four Noble Truths. These are the truth of suffering, the true cause of suffering, the true cessation of suffering, and the true path to that cessation. Since we dislike suffering, we need to think about suffering and what gives rise to it. Unless there is some possibility of gaining complete relief and release from suffering and its causes, then thinking about suffering will be like a headache, only adding to our problems. So it is also of utmost importance that we are aware of the true path and true cessation. These are not just dry philosophical topics; they have a direct bearing on everyday life.

Achieving happiness and overcoming misery is like any other of life's tasks. To be successful we need to gather conducive factors and eliminate obstacles. If we want to achieve social status, fame, and wealth, we have to apply ourselves to create the necessary conditions. In order to become wealthy, we need to be well educated, which in turn depends on material wealth. The health of the mind depends on physical health and vice versa. As I have mentioned before, the mind has primacy over the body, and thus human behavior is determined by the mind. When the mind is not properly disciplined or controlled, all kinds of problems arise.

The root cause of suffering is negative and deluded thought. When animosity and anger are generated, we cause much discomfort to ourselves and great disturbance to others. Therefore, the Buddha has taught us to eradicate negative thoughts and create positive thoughts and actions. This means healthy, rational, and beneficial thoughts and actions. When the Chinese Communists talk about political indoctrination, they are referring to molding people's minds. Unfortunately, they base this on the notion of defeating others and seizing the victory for oneself. Their idea of class struggle is a case in point.

The Buddha by contrast counselled us to help others whenever we can and at the very least to avoid harming them. What we should do is to think about the shortcomings of negative thoughts and actions. At the same time, we should acknowledge the advantages and value of healthy thoughts and actions. It is useful to employ various means and methods to determine the disadvantages of delusions and the benefits of a wholesome mind. When we are convinced of these facts, we will be inspired by a strong interest in creating virtuous thoughts and actions. Similarly, we will develop an inner urge to discard negative thoughts and actions.

The essence of Buddhist teachings can be summarized as the view of interdependence coupled with the conduct of nonviolence. These are the fundamentals I want you to remember. There is no functional phenomenon that exists independently or on its own. All phenomena depend on other factors. Things are interdependent. For example, peace in one nation depends on the attitude of its neighboring countries and the general security in the world. The happiness of one family depends on its neighbors and society at large. Buddhists believe in the theory of dependent origination, not in an almighty creator or in production from no cause at all.

When people forget basic ethical principles and act with a selfish attitude, unpleasant consequences ensue. When you think that your neighbors have nothing to do with your own happiness, you mistreat them. You bully some of them and intimidate and curse others. Can you expect an atmosphere of peace and harmony in such a neighborhood? The answer is obviously no. When you entertain evil thoughts like hostility and hatred, there is no joy in your heart and you are a nuisance to others. On the other hand, if you develop kindness, patience, and understanding, then the whole atmosphere changes. Our text, the "Seven Point Mind Training," says:

First train in the preliminaries.

There are four preliminary practices: thinking about the rarity and potential of life as a free and fortunate human being; reflecting on death and impermanence; thinking about actions and their results; and reflecting on the faults of the cycle of existence. By reflecting on the rarity and potential of life as a free and fortunate human being, you overcome your obsession with the temporal pleasures of this life. By contemplating death and impermanence, you overcome your attraction to favorable rebirths in future lives.

Now, different activities are to be performed during the actual meditation session and during the postmeditation periods. We normally try to concentrate as much as possible during the meditation. If after meditating we leave the mind unguarded and distracted, it will harm our progress; therefore postmeditation practices are recommended.

A meditation session can be divided into the beginning, the actual session, and the conclusion. Traditionally, six preparatory practices are performed at the beginning. First, clean the environment in which you are performing the meditation. You clean it not just for mundane reasons, but also to induce a psychological effect of greater mental clarity. As Po-to-wa said, "Once a meditator has reached an advanced level, every action that he performs can become a stimulus for his practice." So when you clean the place, think of it as a reminder that what actually has to be cleaned is the mind.

Then you can arrange representations of the Buddha's body, speech, and mind in a proper way. Irrespective of what a statue is made of, your attitude toward it should be the same. You should not feel possessive toward it. Followers of the Kadam tradition needed only four images: statues or paintings of the Buddha; those of Avalokiteshvara, who is the embodiment of compassion; those of Tara, who is the embodiment of the Buddha's activities; and those of Achala, a deity who overcomes obstacles.

It is not necessary to have all sorts of different figures, but it is good to have images of the Bodhisattva of

Loving-kindness and of the future Buddha, Maitreya. If you have statues of deities related to your practice, that is good. If you do not, it is not that important, because you should not put too much emphasis on external articles. The emphasis should be placed more on internal development. If you have a lot of beautiful statues in your meditation room, they may look impressive, but if you remain the same short-tempered, scheming, devious person, then it is contradictory. As followers of the Buddha, we should follow what he taught. He taught us to fight the enemy of disturbing emotions within us and to decrease harmful attitudes such as anger. Posing as a follower of the Buddha but acting totally against what he has advised is like insulting the Buddha himself.

To see these images at the moment you wake up in the morning develops a strong determination to follow the Buddha's example. Take them as a reminder to apply the Buddha's instructions. In the evening, regret whatever negative actions you might have committed during the day out of ignorance, and develop a strong resolve not to repeat them. Resolve to correct yourself the next day. This is a proper and beneficial way to relate to religious images.

It would be good also to have a mind training text as a representation of the Buddha's speech. If you have a stupa to represent the mind, fine, but if not, it is not that important. Meditators in the past, like Milarepa, lacked nothing they really needed for their practice, but visiting the places where they have meditated reveals only empty caves. People like us depend so much on external things, like having statues, incense, butter lamps, and so forth, but if these things bring about no effect in the mind, then they are not much help.

A thief once entered Milarepa's cave, and Milarepa rebuked him saying, "How can you find at night things that I can't find in the daytime?" Milarepa was really a great meditator, who due to his effort was able to achieve complete enlightenment within his lifetime. In this context, human beings, Westerners in particular, are generally very shortsighted, expecting quick results. Maybe they are accustomed to things working at high speed because they are used to having so many automatic gadgets. We need to be prepared to put in effort and sacrifice over a long period of time. Our effort and interest should not be just a fleeting obsession but persistent and steady. Milarepa achieved high realizations as a result of his concerted effort and hardship over a long period of time. If we are not prepared to put in such effort and hardship, it will be difficult to achieve what we are looking for. But if we train our minds, we will get to a point where we will see results. It may be difficult, but it is not impossible, so we should not lose courage.

I believe in being practical. I am not impressed only by what happened in the past. I am someone who wants to see practical results now, so I try to put as much effort into the practice as possible. When I compare my state of mind of ten or fifteen years ago with now, I find that a transformation has taken place.

Twenty years ago I used to contemplate emptiness. I was very impressed by the theory of emptiness, and it really inspired me to seek the cessation of suffering. I used to think that once I obtained cessation, I would be able to remain in a blissful state for a long time. I used to think that working for the welfare of other sentient beings, an infinite number of sentient beings, was very idealistic. Later I studied the *Guide to the Bodhisattva's Way of Life* and the *Precious Garland,* and that changed my outlook. Although I still admire the idea of cessation, these days I have a stronger admiration and aspiration for the compassion and tolerance that come with the awakening mind. The union of compassion and emptiness is something quite unique, but you can bring about an inner experience of it if you make the effort.

Sometimes I ask Westerners who have become Buddhists what practical benefit they have derived from it. Some have told me they have noticed a change. After becoming Buddhists there are fewer fights in their families. People are more accommodating and less aggressive. This is one of the direct benefits of changing one's outlook. It creates a more peaceful atmosphere within the family, which in turn affects the mentality of the children. On the other hand, if children are brought up in a very violent community, especially if their parents are always fighting, that will condition the children in a very negative way. This is how the teachings of the Buddha are helpful and effective. Without an initial change taking place within the mind, how can you instantly achieve enlightenment? Enlightenment has to come through a gradual step-by-step process. We should aspire for the ultimate achievement while working in a practical way. I can definitely state that if you undertake the practice, you can bring about a change within the mind.

After having set up representations of the Buddha's body, speech, and mind, you can arrange some offerings, such as food, clean water, flowers, and light. It is said that if you have the right attitude, you will never lack materials for making offerings. So you should make the best offerings you can. In Tibet it was customary to make a feast offering (called *tsok*), and because we would later eat these offerings ourselves, we would make them very nicely. But because we did not have to eat the ritual cake offerings, we would not make them with as much care. For this reason, when we talk of a feast offering we think of something delicious to eat, whereas when we talk about a ritual cake we think of something to be thrown away. That is a mistake. Therefore, when you make offerings, you should do it as best you can. If you cannot afford to do it, then it can be dispensed with. Materials for offering should not be procured by devious means.

Then, having made all these arrangements and washed yourself, take your seat on a cushion that is slightly raised at the back. When it is slightly higher at the back, it makes your spine very straight, which improves your concentration. People who have difficulty sitting cross-legged can sit on chairs, like Maitreya, who was predicted to appear as the future Buddha and is depicted sitting on a throne like a chair.

Meditation means creating a continual familiarity with a virtuous object in order to transform your mind. Merely understanding some point does not transform your mind. You may intellectually see the advantages of an altruistic awakening mind, but that does not actually affect your self-centered attitude. Your self-centeredness will be dispelled only through constantly familiarizing yourself with that understanding. That is what is meant by meditation.

Meditation can be of two types. Analytical meditation uses analysis and reflection, whereas in single-pointed meditation the mind dwells on whatever has been understood. When you meditate on love and compassion, you try to cultivate such an attitude in your mind, thinking, "May all sentient beings be free from suffering." On the other hand, when you meditate on emptiness or impermanence, you take impermanence or emptiness as the object of your meditation.

Here in the practice of mind training, we require preliminary practices like meditation on death and impermanence to urge us into doing the main practice. When you do these meditations, analyze the topic first. Once you have come to a certain conclusion, retain it in your mind and concentrate on it for some time. When you find that you are losing your concentration, again employ analysis. You can carry on with the same round of meditation again and again until you see some kind of effect within your mind. Then, change the pattern of reasons you employ as outlined in texts like the *Guide to the Bodhisattva's Way of Life* or the *Precious Garland* and so forth. This is like trying out different medicines. You may find that some medicines work better than others. If you just go on stubbornly sticking to one round of meditation, it may not be very helpful. You have to put in a lot of effort. This is why study is necessary. Meditation without prior study is like someone trying to climb a rocky cliff without hands.

Now that we have obtained a life as a free and fortunate human being, we have the opportunity to practice the Dharma. Although we must devote a certain amount of time and energy to the affairs of this life, it is important that we also prepare for our future life as well. Otherwise we will waste the opportunities of our precious human existence. If we embark on our next life without having improved ourselves at all, it is almost certain that we will take rebirth in a more difficult realm. If we do that, we will have virtually no chance to engage in the practice of the Dharma, which is essential if we are to attain the fully awakened state of enlightenment. Among the various teachings that the Buddha gave, the chief and the most important are the teachings belonging to the Great Vehicle. The essence of these is the instruction for cultivating the awakening mind. This is the quintessence of the Buddha's words.

Sit on the meditation seat you have arranged. Once again, the most important thing to do is to cultivate the right attitude. Reflect that to be born as a free and fortunate human being is very rare. Ask yourself what is the purpose of rebirth as a human being. We are not born into this world as human beings to create more problems and confusion. If we were, human existence would be worthless. Therefore, the right attitude to adopt is to think you will attain the fully awakened state of a Buddha on the basis of your precious human life. Think that even if you cannot fulfill the needs of other sentient beings, you will not do anything to harm them. It is very important to refresh this kind of motivation right at the beginning of the day so that your motivation, right from when you wake up, is not influenced by disturbing emotions like hatred, anger, and desire. Your attitude from the start should be virtuous. And with that you can clean the place, arrange representations of the objects of refuge, offerings, and so forth.

The most important factor, before you start the actual practice, is to cultivate the right kind of attitude. Your motivation should always follow two themes: taking refuge in the Three Jewels—the Buddha, his teaching, and the spiritual community—and the awakening mind. If your practice is not complemented by taking refuge in the Three Jewels, it will not be a Buddhist practice. If it is not influenced by the awakening mind, it will not be a practice of the Great Vehicle or a cause for achieving the fully awakened state of a Buddha.

In the practice of taking refuge, it is not necessary to visualize the objects of refuge. You can reflect upon their infinite kindness and their great qualities and then imagine taking refuge in them. If you want to visualize the objects of refuge, you can do so according to various traditions. The most important thing is that your practice of taking refuge should be properly founded. The reasons for taking refuge include fear of the sufferings of the cycle of existence, a strong conviction that the Three Jewels have the ability to protect you from these sufferings, and a strong sense of compassion for other sentient beings.

To cultivate the right attitude, it is important to identify what is meant by the Dharma. Dharma means the cessation of suffering and the paths that lead to it. Develop a strong conviction that the Dharma is the true object of refuge that can protect you and all other sentient beings from the fears of the cycle of existence. If you have a powerful understanding of what the Dharma is, it will give rise to a strong conviction within you. That is the true refuge, and you will develop a strong aspiration to achieve such a state.

Having set your mental attitude, recite the refuge formula as much as possible. If you are doing a visualization, you can think of purifying nectar descending from the objects of refuge. It enters you and all sentient beings, purifying you of negativities and placing you all under the protection of the Three Jewels.

Then when you generate the awakening mind, visualize all sentient beings around you. They appear in the form of human beings but continue to undergo the sufferings of the particular realms in which they were born. Ponder these and cultivate strong feelings of compassion for them, wishing that they may be free from their sufferings, and cultivate strong feelings of love, wishing that they may come to possess all happiness. Sentient beings are equal in wishing to find happiness and avoid suffering. Like yourself, they have a right to seek happiness. You cultivate the awakening mind by recognizing this and resolving to work for their well-being. To stimulate and increase the power of your awakening mind, meditate on what are called the four immeasurables: immeasurable love, immeasurable equanimity, immeasurable compassion, and immeasurable joy. Then reflect that although sentient beings desire happiness and wish to avoid suffering, out of ignorance their behavior contradicts their wishes.

So, with awareness of the Buddha's great qualities and the ability of the Three Jewels to protect you from the fears of the cycle of existence, take refuge in them and cultivate a strong determination to achieve the fully awakened state of a Buddha for the sake of all other sentient beings. Such a determination will help increase the force of your awakening mind.

To realize the awakening mind requires a great accumulation of merit. The spiritual master is the most important object for doing this. Think of the spiritual master as the door through which you receive the blessings of the Buddha. If you undertake this practice of refuge and cultivating the awakening mind in connection with a practice of integration with the spiritual master, it will be very powerful. There are many different traditions of such integrating practice in Tibet. In the Kagyu tradition especially, such faith and interest are regarded as the foundation of the path, while in the Geluk tradition, the practice of integration with the spiritual master is regarded as the very life of the path.

On the basis of whatever practice of integration with the spiritual master you decide to do, recite the seven-branch prayer. This includes paying respect, making offerings, openly admitting your misdeeds, rejoicing at the qualities of yourself and others, requesting the Buddhas to teach, beseeching them not to pass away, and dedicating the resultant merit to the welfare of all beings. Offer in visualization, a mandala, a symbolic representation of the entire universe.

Seeking a qualified spiritual master is the first important step in our spiritual life. This is what determines our future spiritual development and attainments. So, before accepting someone as your spiritual teacher, you must examine that person thoroughly. In Tibetan, we usually say, "Don't act like a dog finding a lump of meat." The dog takes no time to think but seizes upon the meat and begins to chew it. You should observe the person first, not just choosing someone with a big title and wide influence. Such factors do not necessarily make someone a good Dharma teacher. A Dharma teacher is our guide on the spiritual path, and, therefore, such a master should practice what he or she preaches. Real guidance can be provided only from the master's own experience and not on the basis of mere intellectual understanding. This is why seeking a qualified master is explained as the root or foundation of Dharma practice.

Tibetans generally tend to have blind faith in anyone with the title of lama. On the other hand, they pay little attention to people who have achieved high realizations through constant practice and hardship but who do not have such a label. This is a bad habit. The person you take as a spiritual master should be someone qualified. He or she should at least be gentle and have tamed his or her own mind, because the very purpose of adopting someone as your spiritual master is to tame the mind. This means that the spiritual master should be someone who has achieved realizations through constant practice.

It is common knowledge that to achieve the desired results, it is essential to gather the conducive factors and eliminate obstacles. We plan in advance, whether we are working on developments in science and technology or economics or any other area. When we follow the steps we have laid out, we are almost certain to achieve the result we are aiming for. Since the purpose of Dharma practice is ultimately to achieve enlightenment, we must be very careful how we plan and implement our course of our action. Therefore, it is very important to find a suitable and qualified spiritual teacher.

Since the spiritual master plays a crucial role in our quest for realization, the Buddha has defined his or her qualifications at great length. To summarize a spiritual master's essential qualities: the person should be true to his or her practice and rich in knowledge of the Dharma. Therefore, it is essential that we examine a potential spiritual master before establishing a master-disciple relationship with that person. It is absolutely fine to listen to his or her teachings, for such contact will provide us with firsthand experience of the person's teaching ability. To evaluate the person's personal practice, we can examine his or her lifestyle. We can also learn about the person from people who already know him or her. It is also useful to get to know the person in other contexts. So when you feel confident, you should then seek to adopt that person as your spiritual master.

Once you have accepted someone as your spiritual master, it is essential to cultivate a proper sense of faith and respect and abide by his or her spiritual instructions. It is important to be clear that faith and respect do not imply blind faith. On the contrary, there should be a more informed approach. In the sutras the Buddha explains that a disciple should abide by the spiritual master's virtuous instructions but disregard his or her unwholesome commands. The texts on discipline follow a similar line, stating that you should not accept anything a teacher suggests that does not accord with the Dharma.

The main criterion for deciding whether a teacher's instruction is acceptable or not is whether it conforms to fundamental Buddhist principles. When it does, we should respectfully obey. Such a teaching is sure to produce positive results. When a teacher's advice contradicts Buddhist principles, we should hesitate and seek clarification. For instance, if an ordained person were told to drink alcohol, it would contradict the vows of ordination. So unless the teacher gave a special reason for doing so, it would be wiser to ignore the teacher's command.

In short, the spiritual master should be proficient in the three trainings in ethics, meditation, and wisdom. This in turn requires an understanding of the three sets of discourses, which implies that he or she should have a knowledge of the scriptures. The spiritual master should be someone who can answer your questions directly and clarify your doubts and whose outward appearance and behavior indicates or complies with inner realization. There is a saying that the stripes of the tiger are visible but those of human beings are not; still, we can infer what other people are like from the way they appear to us.

Having found and developed faith in a spiritual master, it is important to avoid a breakdown in your relationship. So how should you relate to such a being? We can think in this way: "Since the Buddhas are actively engaged in working for the welfare of sentient beings and we are among those seeking liberation, there should be a medium by which we can receive their inspiration and blessing. This is the role of the spiritual master, for it is the spiritual master who brings about a transformation within our minds."

What actually prevents us from cultivating such faith is seeing faults in the spiritual master. In order to counter that, we should reflect that our perception may not always be valid. Our minds are clouded by ignorance and our long association with the habits of ignorance and deceived by the strong influence of our own karmic actions. Until we are able to dispel these clouds, we will not perceive the real nature of our spiritual master, that is, as a Buddha. Buddhas are not accessible to us as they truly are. It is only when they appear as ordinary beings like ourselves that their activities and blessings have meaning for us. Assuming ordinary forms means not only that they do not display all the noble major and minor marks of a Buddha, but also that they possess natural human weaknesses. Assuming such forms is a great kindness and consideration, because it is only in that way that they become visible and accessible to us.

If you are able to overcome the tendency to see faults in your spiritual master through such reflections, you have made great progress. Then begins the process of increasing natural and spontaneous faith in the spiritual master, which serves as the foundation of progress on the path. Without overcoming the tendency to project faults onto the spiritual master, you cannot develop a recognition of him or her as a Buddha. This does not mean blindly following whatever the spiritual master tells you to do. If something is beyond your ability, you do not have to do it. Similarly, if the spiritual master gives you advice that contradicts the general Buddhist mode of behavior, you can explain to him or her why you cannot do it. It is better to do this than cultivate a misunderstanding. If you train your mind in such ways, it is possible to increase your faith in the spiritual master and develop a spontaneous feeling toward him or her.

It is said that developing faith in the spiritual master is like the dawning of the sun on the path to enlightenment. After having developed faith, cultivate deep respect by reflecting upon your teacher's great kindness. The most important aspect of this kindness is that he or she guides us on the path leading to enlightenment. If we read accounts of the past lives of the Buddha, we find that he underwent great hardship to obtain even one verse of teaching. It was the same for great Indian masters like Naropa, who underwent great hardship to obtain instruction from Tilopa, and for Milarepa in relation to Marpa. All the tales about these great personalities testify that the practice of Dharma is not easy. It requires a long, hard effort. The spiritual masters who impart their knowledge to us with care and compassion are taking a great responsibility. If you reflect along these lines, you will be able to see how the spiritual master is the foundation of the achievement of high realizations. Therefore, if you undertake practices of purification and accumulation of merit in relation to the spiritual master, it will be very powerful.

Within the god realms there are many different levels, such as the Joyous Land. This came into existence through the force of Maitreya's great aspiration and merit, so you can visualize him there. It is said that when Atisha and Tsong-kha-pa passed away, they traveled to the Joyous Land of Maitreya. We who practice Buddhism today, have a special connection to this realm. As practitioners who have been able to enter the path and follow the teachings of Buddha Shakyamuni, there is a good chance that we may become enlightened during the era of the next Buddha, Maitreya. You can meditate on your spiritual master as he or she normally appears to you. Visualize him or her in the space before you at the level of your forehead. Alternatively, visualize him or her in the form of Tsong-kha-pa, for example, at the heart of Maitreya. Imagine inviting him from the Joyous Land and that he descends to the space before you. First address your prayers and requests for realization to the spiritual master. Then visualize him or her seated on the crown of your head and begin whatever meditation you are going to do.

In order to reflect on the preciousness of life as a human being, it is necessary to consider the other places where we could have been reborn as a result of our karma. We know that karmic actions leave an imprint on the mindstream or continuity of consciousness. We commit various kinds of actions in relation to external objects, and we accumulate others by entering into a deep state of meditative concentration. Sometimes actions of this latter type result in birth as a god. Even these days I know some people who, although they do not profess to practice the Dharma, have had certain experiences connected to mental development through which they attain a certain amount of mental absorption. This shows that human beings have different aptitudes; some are more involved with external objects, others are more inward looking, tending to be more concerned with inner realizations and absorptive states of mind. Just as there are many different aspects of consciousness, so there are different types of existence.

When the mind is untamed, it may be likened to the animal realm. The level of untamed mind in which you experience the most intense suffering can be likened to the hell realm. On the other hand, the mind can be trained. The highest point of that training is the fully awakened state of enlightenment. It is difficult to prove the existence of different realms as they are explained in the scriptures, because they tend to contradict observed facts. However, the Buddha himself said that when something contradicts experience and logic it should be abandoned.

It is difficult to prove assertions in the scriptures that the hell realms exist at a certain depth under the Indian continent. But we can definitely say that among human beings there are different kinds of mentality. Some people are tortured by intense suffering and anxiety. Even animals experience different types of existence. There are also certain mysterious forces, which we attribute to spirits. Among the different realms of existence, such as the gods, human beings, and animals, the higher or more fortunate forms include the human and god realms.

Reflect on the great rarity and potential of human existence. Apply the same type of practice when you meditate on the next topic, death and impermanence. Make fervent requests to the spiritual master to be able to achieve realization through your meditation and to overcome obstacles to your doing so. This is how you should proceed through all the other meditations concerned with this practice. At the end of your meditations, the spiritual master, whom you have been visualizing before you, dissolves through your crown aperture and comes to rest at your heart. Develop a strong conviction that you have received the inspiration of the spiritual master's body, speech, and mind. The text mentions the eight-petaled lotus of the heart, but that does not mean the physical heart that pumps blood. When we say that someone courageous is stout-hearted, we are not referring to any physical qualities of his or her actual heart. Here the eight-petaled lotus of the heart refers to the mind, because we sometimes identify the mind with heart. You should visualize the spiritual master seated within what we call the central channel.

There are certain channels within our body, some of which are visible and some of which are very subtle and cannot be seen. Various texts explain that when we undertake certain tantric techniques involving visualization of channels and we actually focus on the vital points of the body, it has a physical effect. This shows that the channel or vital point is present, even though it may not be visible in the physical sense. You can visualize what is known as the indestructible drop within the channel wheel at your heart. When the spiritual master dissolves through the crown of your head, you should visualize him or her becoming absorbed into the indestructible drop at your heart. Imagine that he or she becomes inseparable from your own mind and that you receive inspiration.

The Tibetan word for inspiration actually means "force of transformation," implying that the virtuous qualities of the object transform the nature of your mind. When we seek blessings, in the Buddhist sense, we are seeking a transformation within our minds. So if we have been able to transform our minds, we will have actually received the spiritual master's blessing in the true sense of the word. Otherwise it will be just like the story of the owl with the flat head. When someone asked him how his head became flat, he said it was due to constantly receiving his spiritual master's blessings by being patted on the head in a former life.

At the end of the meditation session, however long or short it has been, it is very important to rejoice in what you have done. Then dedicate the positive potential you have gained to the achievement of enlightenment for the sake of all sentient beings. Rejoicing is very important because it increases the force of your merit. Think that all the positive potential you have accumulated during the session is not directed to your own personal gain but only to the welfare of other sentient beings. That is how you dedicate your merit to the achievement of enlightenment for the sake of other sentient beings. In addition, reinforce your practice by recalling your understanding of emptiness. Reflect that all experiences and phenomena are dependent upon causal conditions. Since they lack an independent nature, dedicating your merit and making aspirational prayers will cause all experiences to be of benefit. Reinforcing your practice by recalling your understanding of emptiness can seal what you have achieved during the session.

You should not be like an actor, who puts on a costume for the performance and takes it off immediately at the end. Many of us are like that. Although we undertake the practice very seriously during the meditation session, after it is over, we revert to the same negative person again. We do whatever we like—fighting, quarreling, and so forth. You should neither think nor behave like that. Things are easy during the actual meditation session because there is no one to interfere with you. But once you emerge from your session, you will encounter many external conditions that may harm your practice. At such times it is very important to guard your attention without letting your mind be distracted. Meditation is like recharging your battery. During the actual session you are recharged, but the purpose of recharging your battery is to put it to use. When you meditate, you are trying to transform your mind, but the effect really shows only during the postmeditation period. You should not neglect or conceal the progress you have made during the meditation session but maintain it during your day-to-day life.

At the end of the session, as I explained before, you should dedicate the merit you have created to the welfare of others. That is how you conclude the main meditation session. Afterward you can follow the appropriate behavior when you are eating food, washing, and so forth. If we lead our lives in this way, we will be able to make the entire twenty-four hours of the day virtuous and meaningful, and then the weeks, months, and years will become meaningful, too.

If you are able to practice in this way, you will fulfill one of the maxims of the twelfth- and thirteenth-century Kadampa masters in Tibet. They used to say that at death the best practitioner is delighted, because he is changing his form for a better and more suitable one with which to practice the Dharma. The middling practitioner has no desires but is completely prepared. And even the poorest practitioner has no regrets about having to die. Because of the power of their realization, when they died such practitioners would be able to remain in the state of clear light, in some cases for days. For example, my own late teacher, Kyabje Ling Rinpoche, remained in the state of clear light for thirteen days. In the last days of his life, due to illness, he looked very frail and unwell. But after passing away and remaining in the state of clear light, his complexion regained all its former radiance.

If you practice properly, you can make your life as a free and fortunate human being worthwhile. As the Kadampa masters used to say, "Seek full enlightenment; be prepared to make great effort and undergo hardship and undertake the practice according to whatever is most appropriate at the time."

CHAPTER 4

CREATING THE
PERSPECTIVE FOR
PRACTICE

*Life as a free and fortunate human being is
referred to here as something precious. Such
a human life is found rarely, but individuals*

who possess it can achieve great things because of it.
Yet it is not enduring but fragile and extremely tran-
sient. It is important that we are aware of these characteristics of our lives and then prepare ourselves for
making the best use of them. It is easy to see that
human potential far exceeds the abilities of other living creatures in the world. The human mind has far-
reaching vision. Its knowledge is boundless. Because of
the power of the human mind, new discoveries and in-
ventions abound on our planet. But the crucial thing is
that all these innovations should promote happiness
and peace in the world. In many instances this is not
the case. Unfortunately, too often human ingenuity is

used in a misguided way to create disturbances, disunity, and even war.

The achievements of human intelligence are obvious. The ideas and activities of even a single individual can have far-reaching benefits for millions of people and other living creatures. When our human skills are channeled in the right direction, motivated by a proper attitude, wonderful things happen. Therefore, the value of human life is inestimable. From a more strictly spiritual perspective, it is on the basis of a human life that we can develop different types of insight and realization. Only the human mind can generate infinite love and compassion. Being more concerned about other sentient beings than ourselves and working tirelessly in their interest are among the noble attributes of human nature.

Life as a human being is extremely valuable in terms of achieving both our temporary and ultimate goals. In this context, the temporary goal refers to attaining higher rebirth, and the ultimate goal refers to nirvana and full enlightenment. These goals are precious and difficult to attain. To do so, individuals must be in a position to practice and to accumulate the necessary causes. Only human beings are endowed with the opportunity and intelligence to achieve these goals. If we are to be reborn in the higher realms, we need to refrain from unwholesome actions and practice virtues like generosity and patience. When we engage in right practices, we have the potential to achieve nirvana and Buddhahood.

Once we have gained some conviction that life as a free and fortunate human being is rare and precious, we should reflect that it is not permanent. Although life as a human being has such potential, it is short-lived and does not last. According to the textual instruction, we should meditate here on three fundamental topics: the certainty of death, the uncertainty of when it will occur, and that when death does take place, only the individual's spiritual realization will be of any help. These points can be easily understood and present no intellectual challenge. However, we must meditate on them over and over again until we are deeply convinced. Everyone agrees that sooner or later we all have to die. So the certainty of death is not in question. Rich or poor, young or old, all must die one day. Death is uniform and universal, and no one can either deny or defy this fact of life.

What fools us is the uncertainty of the time of death. Even though we know very well we have to die, we assume that it will be after some time. We all think that we are not going to die soon, and we cling to a false belief that death will not occur for years and years. This notion of a long and indefinite future stretching out ahead of us deters us from serious spiritual endeavor. The whole purpose of meditation on impermanence and death is to move us to engage actively in spiritual practices.

Let me lay out some general guidelines that can help to make our spiritual practice productive and fruitful. Our spiritual pursuit consists, as I have already explained, of meditation sessions and the postmeditation period. People often have the impression that spiritual practices are done only during meditation sessions; they ignore the need for practice during the postmeditation period. It is important to realize that this approach is mistaken. Practice during the postmeditation period is equally important. Therefore, we need to understand how the two kinds of practice complement each other. Spiritual understanding gained in meditation should enhance our understanding during the postmeditation period and vice versa. As a result of the inspiration gained during the meditation sessions, we can develop many virtues like compassion, benevolence, respecting others' good qualities, and so forth. During the session, it is much easier to assume a certain degree of piety. But the real test is when we are faced with the outside world. Therefore, we must be diligent in our practices during the postmeditation period.

When we sit and do our prayers and meditation, we certainly find some peace of mind. We are able to generate compassion toward the poor and needy and feel more tolerant toward our rivals. The mind is more relaxed and less aggressive. But it is really difficult to maintain this momentum when we are confronted with the circumstances of real life. Meditation is like training ourselves for the real world. Unless we engage in a harmonious blend of our experiences of the meditation and postmeditational periods, our spiritual endeavor will lose its much-needed effect. We can be kind and compassionate during our meditation, but if someone harasses us on the road or insults us in public, it is very possible we will become angry and aggressive. We might even retaliate on the spot. If that happens, all the kindness, patience, and understanding we developed in our meditation instantly vanish. Of course, it is very easy to be compassionate and altruistic when we are sitting comfortably on our seats, but the test of the practice is when we encounter a problem. For example, when we have the opportunity to fight and we refrain from fighting, that is Dharma practice. When we have the power to bully someone and we refrain from doing so, that is Dharma practice. So, the real Dharma practice is to control ourselves in such circumstances.

To make our spiritual practice stable and enduring, we must train consistently. A fair-weather practitioner has little hope of achieving his or her goal. It is extremely important to practice the teachings day after day, month after month, and year after year. Anyone who practices consistently can develop spiritual realizations. Since every impermanent phenomenon changes, one day our wild and rough minds will become disciplined and wise, fully relaxed and peaceful. Such wonderful mental qualities can be developed simply by seeing the advantage of virtuous thought and action and the drawbacks of delusion. Nevertheless, it is vital that the practitioner learns the proper technique and method. In the quest for spiritual realization, we do not have to use brute force.

When I was receiving teachings from Khun-nu Lama, he told me a story of someone in Lhasa doing circumambulations. Someone else was meditating there, and the one circumambulating asked, "What are you doing?" The other replied, "I am meditating on patience." The first retorted, "Eat shit!" and the meditator jumped up, shouting in anger. This clearly shows that the real test of practice is whether we can apply it when we encounter disturbing situations. I feel that practice after the session is probably more important than the practice we do during the session. During the session we are actually refueling or recharging our energy to be able to do the practice after the session. Therefore, the more we are able to mold the mind during the session, the better we will be able to face difficulties afterward.

The text explains the nature of the special kind of human life that has the freedom to practice the Dharma. Individuals who have the freedom and opportunity to do Dharma practice are not encumbered by wrong views. They are free from the constraints of birth as an animal, a hungry spirit, or a hell being. They have avoided being born in a place where the Buddha's teaching does not prevail or in a remote barbaric land. Nor have they been born dumb or stupid.

Imagine being born as a bird, concerned only with finding food. We would have no opportunity to practice the Dharma. Fortunately, we have not been born as birds or animals but as human beings. But, even as human beings, we could have been born in a remote land where the Buddha's teaching was unheard of. Wealth and intelligence would make no difference; we would not be able to practice the Dharma. My Western friends come from places where there used to be no practice of Buddhism. But, because of their positive instincts and the changing times, we have been able to meet and share the teachings. At one time, Western lands would have been called remote lands where people were not free to practice. We should appreciate not only that we have been born as human beings, but also that we all now have the conditions necessary for putting the Dharma into practice.

Life as a human being is the most suitable basis for attaining nirvana and Buddhahood. Since we have found such a great opportunity, nothing could be worse than failing to put it to good use. We have found this precious human birth as a result of accumulating great virtue in the past. We must put it to good effect now by continuing to practice the Dharma. Otherwise we will be like the merchants of old who went to great lengths to cross the ocean in search of jewels, only to return empty-handed. This human body is likened to a ship in which we can cross the ocean of suffering of the cycle of existence. Having found it, we have no time to sleep and not do the practice.

Life as a free and fortunate human being is very difficult to find because its cause is difficult to create. Most human beings are involved in unvirtuous activities, and therefore most of us will take inferior rebirths. On the basis of present conduct and behavior, it will be difficult for most of us to be born as human beings in our next lives. And if we do not obtain human life, we will engage only in negative activities, with no opportunity to practice Dharma.

Life as a free and fortunate human being is also rare simply in terms of numbers. If you compare the number of sentient beings in the human realm and those in the realms of animals and so forth, you will find that animals and birds far outnumber human beings. Even when they have obtained life as human beings, very few turn their minds toward Dharma practice. Therefore, we have to generate a wish deliberately to extract meaning from our lives as human beings.

It is clear from what we have discussed here that life as a free and fortunate human being is extremely rare. Those of us who are endowed with all these special features must realize that we have the ability to achieve great goals. Here, where I am teaching the holy Dharma, we are surrounded by countless birds and insects. But, far from understanding these teachings, they have not the slightest thought of virtue. They only think about food. So it is not sufficient that the Dharma be available. Individuals require a working basis that enables them to understand and put the teachings into practice.

Because of the long tradition of Great Vehicle Buddhism in Tibet, Tibetans have acquired certain innate positive qualities. They are given to saying kind and sympathetic words. Even in remote nomadic areas, illiterate Tibetans pray for the sake of all sentient beings, thinking of them all as having been their mothers in past lives. I have met many people from these places, who ask me to come back to Tibet soon for the benefit of all mother sentient beings. It sometimes makes me laugh that they think of motherly sentient beings only in Tibet and nowhere else. Anyway, the important thing is that, because of their compassion, they have strong positive instincts to care for sentient beings.

Buddhism flourished in China in the old days, and Tibetans believed the emperors to be emanations of Manjushri, the Bodhisattva of Wisdom. In retrospect, I think we were naive in our sincerity and failed to gain a reciprocal response. Consequently, we Tibetans have had to suffer. There have been great political upheavals since the Communists took power. They seem to hate Buddhism as if it were poison. Because of indoctrination, the Chinese react to each other with hostility, suspicion, jealousy, and other negative thoughts. During campaigns to eliminate birds and insects for ideological reasons, even children were recruited. Under such circumstances, their natural instincts to be kind and virtuous are suppressed. On the other hand, in Tibetan families every effort is made to instill virtuous imprints in the minds of the young.

Life as a free and fortunate human being can be viewed in various ways. We are not qualified merely by being born as human beings. Imagine being born during what is known as a dark age, when a Buddha has not manifested in the human world. You may possess wealth, power, and influence, but spiritually you will be in the dark. At such times there is no Dharma in the world.

It is important to understand what is meant by practice of the teachings. Different modes and procedures are aimed directly or indirectly at molding the unruly mind and disciplining it, subduing negative aspects of the mind and enhancing its positive aspects. For example, we recite prayers and do meditation. Such practices should promote goodness of heart and foster virtues like kindness and patience. They should subdue and eliminate negative aspects of the mind like animosity, anger, and jealousy, because these are a source of disturbance and unhappiness for ourselves and others. This is why practice of the Dharma is beneficial.

This automatically leads to the question, Is it possible to practice the teachings? The answer is an emphatic yes. At this juncture we have obtained this human life. We have the fortune to have met appropriate spiritual masters who are compassionate and capable in guiding us on the proper path. We also have freedom and opportunity to engage in spiritual practice.

We should not think of postponing our practice of Dharma until the next life. This is a mistake, because it will be difficult to be born as a human being in the future. Nor should we think that we will put off our practice until next year or even next month. That we will die is inevitable, but we do not know when it will be. Of the many practices open to us, generating the awakening mind is the most important.

It is important to remember that everyone innately possesses Buddha nature and that disturbing emotions are only temporary afflictions of the mind. By properly practicing the Dharma, these disturbing emotions can be completely removed, and our Buddha nature will be revealed in all its potential.

All our spiritual practices should be directed toward developing the altruistic thought of the awakening mind. In order for this sublime thought to arise, it is essential to understand sentient beings' plight. This helps us to generate kindness and compassion for others. Unless we have some experience of suffering, our compassion for others will not amount to very much. Therefore, the wish to free ourselves from suffering precedes any sense of compassion for others. The goal of all our spiritual practices should be the awakening mind. This is the supreme and most precious of all the Buddha's teachings. In order that our sense of the awakening mind be effective and powerful, meditate on death and the law of cause and effect. Meditate, in addition, on the vicious nature of the cycle of existence and the benefits of nirvana. All these practices are complementary because they each serve to provoke us into developing the awakening mind.

The second step in developing the awakening mind is to think about death and the impermanent nature of things as well as the disadvantages of not doing so. Thinking about death and impermanence opens the door to achieving excellent qualities in this life and the next. Meditation on death and miseries of the lower realms of existence is of primary concern to those practitioners who are trying to ensure the welfare of their own future lives. They aim to achieve their goals by taking refuge in the Three Jewels and observing the law of cause and effect. Such practitioners principally abstain from the ten unvirtuous actions.

Through the process of meditation, individuals seeking a happy rebirth come to realize that the body is impermanent and subject to decay. It is under the sway of disturbing emotions and past actions, both of which ultimately stem from the ignorant conception of true existence. Whatever arises because of ignorance is miserable by nature. Practitioners who merely seek a happy rebirth chiefly meditate on coarse impermanence, observing that we all die, flowers wither, and houses collapse. Those who seek the peace of nirvana meditate on subtle impermanence, observing that all phenomena are subject to momentary change.

On the other hand, if you do not think about death and simply try to forget it, you will involve yourself only in activities concerned with this life. Even if you pretend to practice the Dharma, you will do it mainly for the benefits of this life. So not remembering death leads to a very limited kind of existence. But thinking about death reminds us of the next life, which reduces our emphasis on the things of this life. Of course, we have to work to maintain our livelihood, but we will not forget the next life. We need to think about death and impermanence because we are too attached to the goods of this life: our possessions, relatives, and so forth. Fear of death, to one who practices the Dharma, does not mean fear of becoming separated from relatives, wealth, or one's own body. From that point of view, fear is pointless because sooner or later we have to die. A more useful fear is the fear of dying too soon, without having been able to do what is necessary to ensure a better future life.

It is common knowledge that death is certain and that no one can avoid it. Instead of disregarding it, it is better to prepare beforehand. Numerous scriptures explain the advantages of remembering death and disadvantages of ignoring it. If we prepare for the eventuality through meditation, when it strikes it will not come as such a shock or be so hard to cope with. If we anticipate trouble in the future, we take precautions. When we are mentally prepared for what might happen, we are not caught unawares when calamity actually befalls us. Thus we meditate on death, not in order to create terror or unhappiness for ourselves, but to equip ourselves to face it when it comes. As long as we remain in the cycle of existence, we will not be free from sickness, old age, or death. Therefore, it is wise to prepare ourselves for what is inevitable. We need to make ourselves familiar with the process by which death occurs and the intermediate state between lives that follows it. If we do so, when we encounter these different events we will be able to face them with determination and courage.

As I said above, in reflecting on death there are three major points to remember. These are that death is certain, that the time of death is unpredictable, and that at the time of death nothing will help except our understanding of the Dharma. The inevitability of death is obvious and goes without saying. Nevertheless, we si.ould reflect on how death occurs in relation to time and place. Not a single individual will avoid death. Death is a universal condition. This has been true in the past, remains so at present, and will continue to be true in the future. Whatever physical existence we adopt will not be immune to death. Even Buddhas have left their bodies behind, so what can be said of ordinary beings?

In terms of place, there is nowhere that can be regarded as a death-free zone. Wherever we stay we cannot avoid death. We cannot hide in the mountains, we cannot remain in space beyond death's reach. Death comes upon us like the falling of a huge mountain from which there is no escape. We may be brave, cunning, and clever, but whatever tactics we use, there is nowhere to escape from death, not high in the mountains, deep in the sea, in the densest forest, or in the crowded city. There is not a single person in history who has not had to die. Even the most spiritually evolved have passed away, not to mention the most powerful kings and the bravest warriors. Everyone, rich and poor, great and small, man and woman, has to die.

When meditating on death, we should pay closest attention to its unpredictability. The uncertainty about when death will strike actually impedes our spiritual endeavors. We accept that death will definitely come one day, but since its time of arrival is not fixed, we tend to think of it always as being some way off. This is an illusory notion. As a matter of fact, we are constantly racing toward our death without stopping even for a moment.

We may be alive today, but sometimes death overtakes us without our finding the time to practice the Dharma. We cannot add something to lengthen our lives. Life continuously and uninterruptedly declines. Years are consumed by months, months are consumed by days, and the day is consumed by hours. Our lives are destroyed as quickly as a drawing on the surface of water. Just as the shepherd drives his flock to the fold, old age and sickness drive us toward death. Because of our physical structure, we are unlikely to live longer than a hundred years. Our life span is defined by our karma. It is not easily extended. Of course, prayers for long life, longevity empowerments, and so forth might enhance one's life to some extent, but it is very difficult to prolong or add to it. Things we did just a few days ago now exist only in our memories. We cannot have these experiences back. This is true even of the experiences we had this morning. Since then, a few hours have passed, which means that our lives are a few hours shorter. Life is ebbing away with every tick of the clock.

As each week follows another, we fail to notice time passing. Sometimes, when I have a vivid recollection of my life in Lhasa, it seems I experienced it only a few days ago. We have been in exile over thirty years, but it is only when we meet old friends from Lhasa or their children that we realize what a long time it has been. We have a tendency to think of the past as something that happened quickly and the future as stretching out into the distance. Consequently, we always tend to think that we still have a lot of time to practice. We think of it as a future project. We are deceived by this negative tendency.

Even while we are alive, we do not have much time to practice the Dharma. Half our lives we spend asleep. The first ten years we are merely children, and after twenty we begin to grow old. Meanwhile, our time is taken up with suffering, anxiety, fighting, sickness, and so forth, all of which limit our ability to practice.

One hundred years from today, not one of us, except the one or two born in the last few days, will still be alive. We have a strange habit of talking about someone dying in a certain place, without thinking that the same death will overpower us. It never occurs to us that we too will die. The television reports people being killed, but we always remain the viewers, not the ones who are going to die. Therefore, thinking about the inevitability of death, we should determine to practice the Dharma, to cease procrastinating by starting today. Of the many levels of practice, meditation on the awakening mind is the most important, so we should resolve to do that now.

In Buddhist cosmology, our planet is referred to as the Southern World. Since we inhabit this world, our life span is extremely uncertain, whereas the life span of beings in the Northern World is said to be definite. It is difficult to take the scriptural description of these worlds literally. What is important about the Buddha's teaching is his explanation of the Four Noble Truths and his instructions on how to transform the mind.

Sometimes I lightheartedly tell people that the Buddha did not come to India to draw the maps of the world. When there is a contradiction between the scientific account and the Buddhist scriptural description of the universe, we should accept what can be observed to be true. There is no need to be dogmatic or narrow-minded about it. This is not to disparage the Buddha's fundamental teachings. Reflecting on these, we can appreciate the vast profundity of the Dharma. What the scriptures do say is that the life span of the beings of our world is extremely unpredictable. Sometimes people die when they are still very young, and sometimes they live into ripe old age.

In our meditation on death we should consider the factors that bring it about. The conditions that sustain life are limited. Ironically, sometimes even these cause death. Food and shelter are among our basic needs, but occasionally bad food or overeating can be fatal. Our bodies are composed of elements, which are by nature opposed to each other. When we talk about good health, we mean that these opposing elements are in proper balance. When that balance is disturbed, we suffer from different ailments. On the outside our bodies seem to be solid and strong, but the human metabolism is so subtle and complex that if something happens to one part of the body it can disrupt the functions of the other organs. The body is like a machine with many delicate components. The heart, for instance, has to beat twenty-four hours a day. It could stop at any time. Then what would we do?

Even at the best of times there is no guarantee that we will not die tomorrow. We may believe that because someone is in perfect health, she will not die for a long time. We may think that because someone else is weak and ill, he will die soon. But these are mere assumptions. There are so many causes and conditions for dying that we do not know when death will strike. You may think that, in the event of an earthquake, you have a very solid house. You may think that, if a fire breaks out, your feet are swift and you will be able to run away. Still, we do not have any guarantee that we can protect ourselves against every eventuality. Therefore, we should take every precaution and prepare to face this unknown situation. We can be sure that our deaths will come; we are only unsure when.

Finally, at the time of death, nothing can help except your Dharma practice. When you die, you have to go alone, leaving everything behind. You may have many wonderful friends and relatives, but at that time none of them can help you. Whoever is dearest to you is absolutely helpless. You may be rich, but wealth cannot help you at the time of death. You cannot take a single penny with you. Instead, it is more likely to be a cause of worry. Your best friend cannot accompany you to your next life. Even a spiritual master cannot take his or her most devoted disciples to the next world. Every one of us has to go alone, propelled by the force of our karma.

I often reflect on my own situation as the Dalai Lama. I am sure there are people who are prepared to sacrifice their lives for me. But when my death comes, I have to face it alone. They cannot help me at all. Even my own body has to be left behind. I will travel to the next life under the power of my own actions. So what is it that will help us? Only the imprints of positive actions left on our minds.

Both positive and negative karmic imprints are deposited on the subtle consciousness. This subtle consciousness is known as the primordial consciousness or clear light, which has no beginning or end. This is the consciousness that came from previous lives and goes on to the next. It is the karmic imprints upon it that give rise to experiences of pain and happiness. When you come to die, only the imprints of your positive deeds will help you. Therefore, while you are alive, and especially when you are young, your mind is fresh, and you are able to do a systematic practice, it is important that you prepare yourself for death. Then you will be able to face it properly when the time comes.

The process of death takes place through the gradual dissolution of your internal elements. If you have made your mind familiar with this process, at the time of death when it actually takes place you will be able to handle it. Similarly, if you have become familiar with meditation on love and compassion and exchanging your happiness for the suffering of other sentient beings, these practices will help you. If you have been a real Dharma practitioner, you will face death contentedly.

Of course, if you believe we have only this present life, then at death everything comes to an end. But if you accept the possibility of future lives, then death is just like changing your clothes. The continuity of the mind goes on. However, as we have no idea what the future holds, it is necessary to engage now in practices that will help us then. Even in this world we need friends and support in times of difficulty. When we have to face the unknown alone we will have only our previous practice to support us.

Now when we talk about Dharma practice, people sometimes misunderstand what it means. So let me put it in perspective. Practicing the Dharma does not mean you have to give up your profession or do away with your possessions. There are various levels of practice according to individual ability and mental disposition. Everyone cannot renounce the world and meditate in the mountains. This is not practical. How long could we survive? We would soon starve. We need farmers to grow food, and we need as well the support of the business community. These people also can practice the teachings and integrate their lives within the bounds of the Dharma. Business people must make profit to earn their living, but the profit should be moderate. Similarly, people in other trades and professions can work honestly and conscientiously without contradicting the Dharma. In this way they can serve the community and help the overall economy.

I usually advise people to devote half their time to the affairs of life and half their time to the practice of the teachings. This, I think, is a balanced approach for most people. Of course, we need the real renunciates who dedicate their whole lives to practice. They are worthy of our respect and veneration. We can find them among all traditions of Tibetan Buddhism. There are many meditating in the Himalayas.

After our deaths we do not disappear; we take rebirth. But we cannot be confident that our rebirths will not be in miserable circumstances. We do not take birth voluntarily; we are compelled to do so through the force of our actions. Our actions are of two kinds, positive and negative. If we are to ensure our future well-being, it is important to cultivate wholesome actions. Because existence as an animal, hungry spirit, or inhabitant of hell is extremely miserable, practitioners aspire to attain a more fortunate rebirth. The principal way to fulfill this wish is to abstain from the ten unvirtuous actions. These ten misdeeds include three physical activities— taking life, taking what is not given, and abusive sexual behavior; four verbal activities—lying, slander, harsh words, and idle gossip; and three mental activities— covetousness, malice, and wrong view. Abandoning these ten is crucial if we want to achieve a fortunate rebirth.

The practice of this kind of morality should be understood within the context of the law of karma or action. Every action is bound to produce results. This means that whatever positive or negative activities you do, you will experience similarly positive and negative results. Whatever actions you do will follow you just like the shadow of a bird flying in the sky. Actions also have the potential to increase and multiply. Even if you do a small positive or negative action, the eventual result can be tremendous. You should not think that a particular misdeed is insignificant and will not harm you in the future. Just as a large vessel is filled by drops of water, even minor negativities will harm you later. If you have not performed an action, you will not have to face its result, yet once an action has been done, its effects will never merely disappear. This means that you will have to face its results.

Reflecting on this, you should cease all negative activities and make an effort to accumulate wholesome deeds. Of these, the most important is training in the precious awakening mind, aspiring to attain enlightenment for the benefit of all sentient beings. At the same time, we must appreciate that the workings of karma are subtle and difficult to understand. The subtle play of action and result is extremely difficult to understand, and we may not be able to use our reason at all. Thus our only recourse is to depend on the explanation of someone with experience. If we are to rely on that, we first have to verify that that person is authentic and trustworthy. We can do this by observing his or her conduct and examining those of his or her teachings that we can understand. Satisfying ourselves of their validity is grounds for regarding the teacher as trustworthy.

In our daily lives we see many things directly and can understand them immediately. We can say that this is a peach tree or that is a banana tree without having to use reason or rely on a trustworthy authority.

However, when something is behind me, I do not see it directly with my eyes. But if I hear the mewing of a cat, because of my familiarity with cats I can reason that there is a cat behind my seat. There are also partially obscure phenomena that we cannot perceive directly through our senses but that we can infer on the basis of certain marks or indications. For example, my birthday falls on the fifth day of the fifth month of the Tibetan calendar. This is not something I can discover for myself. I simply have to rely on what my parents have told me. I know that they have no reason to lie about it and were of sound mind. I can safely trust their word, even though I cannot see the matter directly or reason about it.

Now, the subtlest workings of actions and their results or karma are extremely difficult for the human mind to understand. Ordinary people like us cannot comprehend such extremely obscure phenomena either by direct perception or by way of reasoning. No amount of analysis and examination can help us here. We have to depend on someone who has knowledge and experience of these phenomena, such as Buddha Shakyamuni. We do not do so merely by saying that he is great or he is precious. We depend on his words. This is justified because a Buddha does not lie; he possesses great compassion and the omniscient mind, which is the result of eradicating all mental defilements and obstructions. The Buddha's loving-kindness is unconditional and universal. His sole mission is to help sentient beings in whatever way is useful. In addition to his universal compassion, the Buddha is endowed with the wisdom directly apprehending emptiness. These attributes of compassion and wisdom qualify the Buddha as an authentic teacher. He is someone on whom we can rely when our own reason fails.

The ethical discipline of abstaining from the ten unwholesome actions is the actual refuge that protects us from falling into unfortunate states of existence. This practice is sustained by faith in karma or the law of cause and effect. Such faith is acquired by trusting in the words of the Buddha. This is why we have to establish that he is reliable and trustworthy, which we do by examining his teachings. The Buddha's doctrine is vast and profound. His fundamental teachings of the Four Noble Truths are impeccable. Their relevance and validity are beyond question. His explanation of self-lessness as a method for achieving nirvana and Buddhahood is lucid and rational. Analyzing these teachings through logical reasoning will cause our faith and respect to grow.

We can classify human beings into three major categories: those who believe in religion, those who are against it, and those who are uncommitted. The majority fall into the third category. Such attitudes reflect people's different ways of achieving their own well-being. There are those who rely on material comfort and those who rely primarily on spiritual satisfaction.

The Communist Chinese are against religion in general and Buddhism in particular. They denounce religion as a poison, claiming that it harms economic growth and is a tool of exploitation. They even say that religion is an empty and meaningless pursuit. Tibetans, on the other hand, believe in the Buddha's teaching and see it as a source of peace and happiness. Broadly speaking, Tibetans are indeed happy, peaceful, and resilient in the face of difficulties. Those who oppose religion tend to be more anxious and narrow-minded. It is also noticeable that Tibetans do well without having to work so hard, while the Chinese struggle much harder to survive.

Positive, meritorious activity results in happiness and success. The forces involved in the law of cause and effect are not physical entities, but if we observe them carefully we can learn how they operate. When we Tibetans became refugees, our lives were initially very hard. We possessed not an inch of land and had to depend on others for support. In the course of time, our situation improved. This is our good karma coming to fruition. Similarly, in ordinary life some people are more successful than others for no obvious reason. We just say that he or she is lucky, but these are instances of the working of positive karma.

We should stop not only all negative activities, but also the motivation that gives rise to them. It is important to refrain from the ten unwholesome deeds both from a spiritual point of view and because they are contrary to acceptable human behavior. Wanton slaughter of animals, killing human beings, and abusive sexual behavior like rape are against the law everywhere. Nowadays we see many new laws being made, but whatever punishments are prescribed, people always seem to find ways of escaping them. Unless there is a sense of propriety and restraint on the part of individuals, it will be difficult to maintain peace and tranquillity in society. A sense of shame and conscience is more effective than the threat of falling foul of the police and risking punishment. If we have a spiritual practice that provokes a real transformation within the mind, we will not have to depend on external forces. If there is control within individuals' minds, there will be discipline and peace throughout society.

Therefore, we should all try to avoid the ten unwholesome deeds throughout our lives and at least try to avoid engaging in them frequently. We should be especially careful about killing. If you kill even a small insect with great anger, attachment, or ignorance, it can serve to propel you into an unhappy rebirth. Even if you manage to be reborn as a human being, you will tend to have a short life and to be inclined to kill again. In this way you will constantly accumulate negative activities and so will have negative experiences for many lives to come. You can see evidence of this in small children who, even when they are only two or three years, are very fond of killing insects. They have strong imprints left on their minds, resulting in this tendency to kill.

When we are young we are more susceptible to recalling our actions and experiences from previous lives, before they are overlaid by present experience. As we grow up these vivid experiences, whether they are positive or negative, begin to decrease. Later, even though we may not have a vivid memory of it, the force of our actions still lingers in the mind. Likewise, even though we may not later remember certain actions we performed in the early part of our lives, they still retain their potential. A single negative act is not negative only at the time it is done; later it can propel us into a miserable state of existence, where we encounter unceasing suffering.

If you think about this you will take more care. When you appreciate the drawbacks of killing, you will try to avoid doing it. Even when you are bothered by a mosquito and you feel you have a reason to kill it, try to refrain from doing so. You may not be able to donate blood, but at least refrain from shedding it. Of course, it is not that easy, as I know from my own experience. When the mosquito bites you for the first time you may be patient with it. But the second time you become a little more agitated, and when it does it a third time you start to think of killing it.

It is important to think about the faults of killing. Then if you have the opportunity to kill someone but refrain from doing so, you will really be practicing the virtue of not killing. If you say you are avoiding killing when you are not actually in a position to kill, it does not mean very much. A result of not killing is that in the future you will take a better rebirth, such as that of a human being. Your life will be long and you will have a natural dislike of killing and will avoid taking other beings' lives. Actions not only give rise to positive or negative experiences in this life but have a similar effect in future lives.

If we examine our present behavior and mental disposition, we can easily conclude that we have engaged in negative activities in the past. We can also easily see what kind of activities we are more familiar with on the basis of our present experience. Some people who must have become quite accustomed to saying their morning prayers have no difficulty in doing so now. But for those of us without such habituation, it is very difficult to sit and do our prayers daily. Even those among us who are ordained and have been practitioners for years are still easily carried away by disturbing emotions. This shows that we have performed negative activities in the past.

The way to purify these negativities is to call to mind whatever negative activities you have done and openly admit them. To do this you can take refuge in the Three Jewels and generate the awakening mind. Then, with a sense of regret for whatever unwholesome deeds you have done, promise never to repeat them in the future and to engage persistently in spiritual practice. You should continue doing this until you receive a clear indication, for example in your dreams, that your unwholesome deeds have been purified.

Unless you make an attempt to think about the sufferings of the cycle of existence, you will not generate an aspiration for liberation. And unless you think about how you fall into the cycle of existence, you will not understand the method for putting an end to it. You should meditate on the sufferings of the cycle of existence in general as well as those of specific realms of existence. There is no certainty in the cycle of existence. Sometimes, because of the changes of rebirth, your friend becomes your enemy and your enemy becomes your friend, your father becomes your son and your mother becomes your spouse, and so forth. Nothing is certain, so you do not know who is your real enemy and who is your real friend. Even in this life there is no certainty. We call someone who makes us happy a friend. We regard wealth and friends as trustworthy sources of happiness, but if we think more deeply, they are unreliable because they are subject to change.

Lack of satisfaction is one of our greatest sufferings. We enjoy a certain level of wealth or experience in the hope that it will give us some satisfaction, but satisfaction eludes us. The more we enjoy something, the more we desire something else. We see many people surrounded by wealth and attention who still have no contentment. And when they feel deprived of satisfaction and contentment, they think they are the most miserable people in the world. Until we really experience the cycle of existence as just a series of ups and downs, our spiritual practice will not be successful.

We also have to give up our bodies again and again, being born again and again, undergoing the highs and lows of our changing lives. At one point we may be born as kings of a celestial realm, but in our next lives we might fall to a state of unbearable suffering. Whatever wealth we accumulate we must finally leave behind. However respected our names, however widespread our fame, and however great our wealth, we will eventually have to give them up. Whatever has come together must finally part. We wish to enjoy life with our friends and relatives, but in the end we all have to part.

When you die you go alone, and the only light to accompany you derives from the spiritual practice or positive acts you have done. Thus the cycle of existence is unreliable. It is unreliable because you have to give up your body again and again, you cannot rely on receiving help or harm from others, you cannot rely on finding prosperity, and you cannot rely on your companions. No matter how much you enjoy life's pleasures, there is no contentment. Because you have entered the womb over and over again, your series of births is untraceable, which indicates that you have been wandering in the cycle of existence for a beginningless time.

Now let us think about the drawbacks of the human world that we actually experience. It is characterized by the sufferings of birth, sickness, old age, and death. There is no one who can escape these miseries. We have no memory of how we suffered at birth, and the sufferings of our own old age are equally elusive. The Kadampa masters used to say that it is good that old age only comes upon us gradually. If it were to occur all at once—if we were to wake up one morning suddenly wrinkled, bent, and white haired—the shock would be unbearable.

All these sufferings originate from our sense of desire, aversion, and other disturbing emotions. Ignorance is the root of them all. People are born due to the force of karma and disturbing emotions. Therefore, far from being a good beginning, birth is just the beginning of a long stream of suffering. From this point of view, it is ironic that we celebrate birth as something special and continue to observe the birthday every year. Because we are born under the sway of karma and disturbing emotions, we are controlled by many negative forces. How then can we expect to find joy and happiness? We are all like the Tibetans who are under the control of the Communist Chinese. Under such oppressive authority, which shows no respect for the law of cause and effect and which has no mercy, no sense of shame or decency, how can they enjoy peace and happiness?

The suffering of old age creeps up on us, so we hardly notice it. In fact, aging starts from the very moment we are born. It attacks us gently, and although old age is not pleasant, its gradual onset makes it bearable. At the age of twenty we enter adulthood. When we reach about forty, some of our hair turns white and some more of it falls out. Curiously, these are regarded as signs of maturity and dignity. Because aging is not very obvious, we do not see where it is leading. One important thing to remember is that aging is part of our physical makeup. It is not something imposed from outside. So long as we have this contaminated body, we will be subject to the sufferings of birth, old age, sickness, and death. The most intelligent and effective means of overcoming such misery is to eliminate its cause.

These days advanced medical science ascribes many of the causes of sickness to external agents such as bacteria and viruses. But the fundamental cause lies with our physical makeup. Our bodies are susceptible to sickness. All our physical and mental components, including our bodies, are the products of contaminated actions and disturbing emotions. Therefore, our ailments have both physical and mental aspects. We suffer because that is the nature of our bodies. But there is no point in developing a dislike for our bodies. The wisest strategy is to find the causes of suffering and eliminate them. So long as we are under the control of disturbing emotions, real happiness will be hard to find.

The purpose of meditating on suffering is not to cause more anxiety but to inspire us into eradicating its causes. Practice of meditation on the true path leads to the cessation of sufferings and their causes. From this point of view, an intelligent person can see the unfathomable wisdom of the Buddha's beginning his teachings with the Four Noble Truths. Appreciating the merits of nirvana and the drawbacks of the cycle of existence naturally stimulates an individual to engage in practices like the three trainings in ethics, concentration, and wisdom. This is the path that can deliver us to the state of liberation.

The altruistic thought of the awakening mind is the gateway to the Great Vehicle. It literally refers to expanding or extending the mind. By and large, we are usually preoccupied with our own interests and welfare. However, those interests concern only one individual, no matter how important. Other beings are infinite in number, and therefore their interests and welfare are far more important than those of a single individual. When you generate the awakening mind, you extend your care and concern to the well-being of everyone else. The aspiration to attain the fully awakened state of a Buddha for the sake of all sentient beings is a pure and powerful intention. As a result, both others and ourselves will enjoy lasting peace and happiness.

It is important to be aware that disturbing emotions and the obstructions to complete knowledge are but adventitious stains on the mind. They are not intrinsic to the nature of the mind and therefore can be completely removed. The import of this is that omniscience is something we can achieve. Naturally, if we have achieved omniscience, we are in the best position to help others. In trying to be helpful, mere sincerity and dedication are not enough. It is essential to understand each individual's interest and capacity and mental disposition. Then our efforts to fulfill sentient beings' welfare will be effective, and we will able to gradually lead them to Buddhahood.

The awakening mind is the most supremely positive thought. It is worth employing every means and method to generate it. Even in our ordinary everyday life, kindness and good-heartedness are highly valued. This is obvious even in relation to animals like dogs and cats. Kinder, more peaceful dogs attract a better response than those that are aggressive. The same applies in human society. We all like to be around kind people. Their peaceful and relaxed nature is soothing and joyful.

When the head of the family is kind and broad-minded, the rest of the family enjoys peace of mind. Disputes and arguments naturally occur, but when dealt with on the principle of forgiving and forgetting, they cease to be so disruptive. Under the circumstances, such a family is bound to enjoy peace and prosperity. When an aggressive, narrow-minded, and selfish person is head of the family, the reverse is true. Even on an individual level we all appreciate those who are kind and openhearted. If we hold grudges against our fellow beings, we naturally become suspicious of them. This leads to a vicious circle of hatred. Can we expect to enjoy peace and happiness under such circumstances?

Human beings are not intrinsically selfish, because selfishness is a form of isolation. We are essentially social animals depending on others to meet our needs. We achieve happiness, prosperity, and progress through social interaction. Therefore, a kind and helpful attitude is the source of happiness. And the awakening mind is supreme among all such beneficial thoughts. This is what motivates an individual to seek the inconceivable qualities of a fully awakened Buddha in order to benefit infinite sentient beings. This precious thought underpins the noble deeds of the bodhisattvas, the awakening champions embarked on the path to enlightenment. Therefore, realizing the value of the awakening mind, we should make it the central theme of our practice.

CHAPTER 5

THE AWAKENING MIND

The only entrance to the path of the Great Vehicle is generation of the awakening mind. Within the Great Vehicle there are

only two vehicles, the sutra vehicle and the tantra vehicle. Whichever you wish to enter, the only entrance is with the awakening mind. When you possess the awakening mind you belong to the Great Vehicle, but as soon as you give it up you fall away from it. The moment you generate the awakening mind, even if you are bound in the sufferings of the cycle of existence, you will become an object of respect even for the Buddhas, who are themselves awakened. Just as a fragment of diamond is an excellent jewel that surpasses all other ornaments, the diamondlike awakening mind even when it is weak outshines all the qualities possessed by those pursuing personal liberation. Nagarjuna says in his *Precious Garland* that if you wish to attain the unsurpassable state of supreme enlightenment, its source is the awakening mind. Therefore, generate an awakening mind as stable as the king of mountains.

Those who have not developed the awakening mind cannot enter into the secret practice of tantra. Access to tantric teachings is restricted to those who have received initiation and empowerment, and if you do not possess the awakening mind you cannot receive tantric initiation. This is a clear statement that entrance to the secret vehicle also depends on possessing the awakening mind.

The awakening mind is like a seed for the attainment of Buddhahood. It is like a field in which to cultivate all positive qualities. It is like the ground on which everything rests. It is like the god of wealth who removes all poverty. It is like a father protecting all bodhisattvas. It is like a wish-fulfilling jewel. It is like a miraculous vase fulfilling all your wishes. It is like a spear vanquishing the foe of disturbing emotions. It is like armor shielding you from improper thoughts. It is like a sword beheading the disturbing emotions. It is like an ax felling the tree of disturbing emotions. It is like a weapon staving off all kinds of attack. It is like a hook to draw you out of the waters of the cycle of existence. It is like the whirlwind that scatters all mental obstacles and their sources. It is like the concentrated teaching encompassing all the bodhisattvas' prayers and activities. It is like a shrine before which everyone can make offerings.

Therefore, having found this precious life as a free and fortunate human being and come across the complete teachings of the Buddha, we should treasure the awakening mind. What makes the Tibetan Buddhist tradition so valuable is that it includes precious techniques for generating the awakening mind. The existence of this tradition of cultivating love and compassion and developing concern for the welfare of other sentient beings is extremely fortunate. I myself feel extremely fortunate to be able to explain such teachings at times like these. Likewise, you are extremely fortunate to be able to read about such an invaluable attitude.

We should not think of the awakening mind merely as an object of admiration, something to pay respect to. It is something we should generate within ourselves. We have the ability and option to do so. You may have been a horribly selfish person in the earlier part of your life, but with determination you can transform your mind. You may become like the person described in a prayer, who "never expects to work for her own purpose, but always works for the benefit of others."

As human beings we have intelligence and courage. Provided we use them, we will be able to achieve what we set out to do. I personally have no experience of the awakening mind, but when I was in my thirties I used to reflect on the Four Noble Truths and compare the possibility of attaining liberation and developing the awakening mind. I used to think that attaining liberation for myself was possible. But when I thought about the awakening mind, it seemed quite far off. I used to think that even though it was a marvelous quality, it would be really difficult to achieve.

Time has passed and I have entered my forties and then my fifties, and even though I still have not developed the awakening mind I feel quite close to it. Now

I think that if I work hard enough I may be able develop it. Hearing and thinking about the awakening mind make me feel happy and sad at the same time. Like everyone else, I too experience negative emotions like anger, jealousy, and competitiveness, but due to repeated familiarity I also feel that I am getting closer to the awakening mind. It is a unique quality of the mind that once you get familiar with a particular object, your mind gains stability in relation to it. Unlike physical progress, which is subject to natural restrictions, the qualities of the mind can be developed limitlessly. The mind is like a fire, which, if you continually feed it, will become hotter. There is nothing that does not get easier with familiarity.

The first step in actually developing the conventional awakening mind, which is concerned with the interests of others, is to appreciate the faults of self-centeredness and the advantages of cherishing others. A principal practice for developing this awakening mind is the practice of exchanging oneself with others. There are different explanations about how to engage in this practice. In all the explanations, one factor is common: it is necessary at the outset to regard sentient beings with affection. We should think of them as pleasing and attractive and try to cultivate a strong sense of affection for them. This requires generating a sense of equanimity that regulates our fluctuating emotions toward other sentient beings.

To do this it is very helpful to visualize three people in front of you: one who is your relative or friend, another who is an enemy, and someone toward whom you feel neutral. Observe your natural reaction to them. Usually we are predisposed to feel close to our relatives, distant from our enemies, and indifferent to everyone else. When you think about your friend you feel close to her and immediately have a sense of concern for her welfare. When you think about your enemy you immediately feel uncomfortable and ill at ease. You might even be pleased if he were to run into difficulties. When you think about the person toward whom you feel neutral, you find you do not really care whether that person is miserable or happy. You feel indifferent. When you recognize such fluctuating emotions, ask yourself whether they are justified. If you imagine your friend doing you harm, you will find that your reaction to her will change.

Those whom we call our friends in this present life have not been our friends forever. Neither have those we presently think of as enemies been hostile forever. This person who is a friend or relative in this lifetime could have been our enemy in a past lifetime. Similarly, the person whom we regard as an enemy now could have been one of our parents in a previous life. Therefore, it is foolish only to be concerned about those we think of now as friends and to disregard those we think of as enemies. The aim here is to reduce attachment toward your relatives and friends while reducing anger and hatred toward your enemies. Reflect that there is no sentient being who has not been your friend. This is how you cultivate equanimity toward all other sentient beings.

It is also only in relation to other sentient beings that we can observe pure ethics, such as abstaining from killing, stealing, and sexual abuse. None of the ten virtuous actions can be undertaken except in relation to other sentient beings. Similarly, we can cultivate the practice of generosity, ethics, and patience only in relation to other sentient beings. Only in relation to them can we develop love, compassion, and the awakening mind. Compassion, for example, is a state of mind that comes about when we focus on the sufferings of other sentient beings and cultivate a strong wish that they be free from such sufferings. Therefore, without other sentient beings as the object, we would be unable to cultivate compassion.

All the realizations we achieve on the path are dependent upon other sentient beings. Although sentient beings themselves may not intend to help us achieve such realizations, that is not a reason not to value them. For example, we value and seek nirvana by pursuing the path, but neither the path nor nirvana have any intention of helping us. What is more, it is sometimes the case that beings with actively hostile intentions can help us to the highest realizations. Enemies are very important, because it is only in relation to them that we can develop patience. Only they give us the opportunity to test and practice our patience. Not your spiritual master, your friends, or your relatives give you such a great opportunity. The enemy's antagonism would normally arouse your anger, but by changing your attitude you can transform it into an opportunity to test and practice patience. This is why the enemy is sometimes described as the greatest spiritual friend, because he affords us not only the opportunity to practice patience, but also to develop compassion.

Kindness is not confined to our friends and relatives; it is common to all sentient beings. Even when they have not been our mothers, all sentient beings have been kind directly or indirectly. The food, clothing, and shelter we enjoy in this life are possible only due to the kindness of sentient beings. We survive only due to the kindness of sentient beings. Our very birth was dependent upon the kindness of our parents. All the facilities we enjoy are due to the work of many sentient beings. They did not come about spontaneously as if we had discovered a hidden treasure.

Even the accomplishments of this life—fame, wealth, and friends—can be achieved only in dependence on other sentient beings. Fame depends on other people being aware of us; we cannot be famous in an empty, barren land. We need to appreciate that the kindness of sentient beings is not confined to when they have been our parents or friends; it extends to when they have been our enemies as well. This is something to be pondered deeply. It will serve as a great inspiration for cultivating compassion. When you recollect the special kindness of sentient beings in this way, your wish to repay them will be much stronger. You should ask yourself if it would be proper to neglect them now. The natural desire to repay their kindness gives rise to love, compassion, and the superior intention. This eventually results in the awakening mind.

After regarding other sentient beings with affection, we actually have to equate ourselves with others. This is the equanimity that sees all other sentient beings as equal to us because they desire happiness and wish to avoid suffering. The parts of our body—our head, hands, feet, and so forth—are distinct parts, yet we naturally regard them as parts of the whole and do not discriminate among them. Similarly, sentient beings are infinite and of many different varieties. Some help and some harm, but from the point of view that they wish for happiness and shun suffering, they are equal. That is how we cultivate equanimity. So, just as we have always tried by all means to establish our own well-being and happiness, now on the basis of this equanimity, we should try to benefit all sentient beings without partiality or feelings of closeness to some and distance from others. This is something worth doing, as this verse explains so well:

> As no one desires even the slightest suffering
> Nor is ever content with the happiness he has,
> There is no difference between myself and others:
> Therefore, inspire me to rejoice when others are
>   happy.

We encounter suffering and misfortune. We suffer the worse states of rebirth and the sufferings of birth, aging, sickness, and death that afflict human beings. All these sufferings and misfortunes result from the undisciplined state of mind that is derived from self-centeredness. How is this? Because we are preoccupied with our own selfish welfare alone, we neglect the happiness of others and overlook their efforts on our behalf. Instead we kill, steal, and commit rape and adultery, we engage in rumormongering, covetousness, malice, and wrong view. The more self-centered we are, the more we ignore other people and the more susceptible we are to deceiving and bullying them. Even in the case of wrong view there is a great deal of selfish pride. We think of nothing but ourselves, and as soon as something does not conform to our preconceptions we reject it saying, "I don't believe that." Self-centeredness is the basis for the ten unvirtuous actions. Consequently, all the faults of this and future lives are due to our self-centered attitude. Therefore the text says,

Banish the one who is to blame for everything.

We encounter countless sufferings we do not want and are unable to achieve success in what we desire. Without recognizing self-centeredness as the cause, we always pinpoint some external factor. Our taking birth in states of existence where we encounter unending suffering does not happen without causes and conditions. Unfavorable causes arise from actions and disturbing emotions. Actions arise mainly because of disturbing emotions. And among the disturbing emotions, it is the ignorance that clutches onto a misconception of self that is the source of all suffering. Therefore, all the harm, suffering, and fear in the world arise from the misconception of self. Of what use is this great ghost residing within me?

Those of us under the sway of disturbing emotions instinctively hold ourselves dear. We value the self-centeredness and misconception of self within us. We need to examine whether this natural feeling of looking after our own good is beneficial or harmful. What we seek is happiness for ourselves, but as long as we are under the influence of self-centeredness, what we gain is suffering. The self-centered attitude and misconception of self, which function together like two great friends, actually operate against our own interests.

The misconception of self leads to a self-centered attitude residing peacefully at the very core of our being. Our consequent lack of consideration for others is like a sharp weapon of wrong views with which we cut off concern for good and bad deeds. In this way we kill off the possibility of attaining a better rebirth, liberation, or enlightenment. Wrong view arises because of our strong feeling of an intrinsically existent self. Because of that we ignore others, even to the point of ignoring the teaching of the Buddha and deriding the Buddha himself. This is due to our misconception of self. It is like having an evil butcher residing within us. This selfish thought holding a bag of desire, aversion, and ignorance is like a thief within who robs us of our crop of virtue.

The seeds of consciousness are planted in the fields of action. They are irrigated again and again with the waters of desire and craving by the farmer within us who cultivates the shoots of the states of rebirth. This, too, is because of our self-centered attitude. Although countless Buddhas and bodhisattvas have appeared in the past, we have been unable to develop a single one of their qualities. Because of the self-centeredness within us we remain naked, empty-handed, and slothful. Wherever we stay in the cycle of existence we are beset by suffering. Whoever we associate with is a friend of suffering. Whatever we enjoy is an object of anguish. Even though the Buddha has made this clear, still, filled with covetousness, we think only of accumulating wealth because of our self-centered attitude.

Not knowing whether something is good or bad, we entertain unnecessary expectations and doubts about it because of our self-centeredness. We go to war and risk losing our lives, thinking that somehow we will survive and live to fight another day, because of our self-centeredness. Faced with the slightest problem, we always blame our abbot or teacher, friend, or parents. Our sense of self-centeredness is shameless. We are jealous of our superiors, competitive toward our equals, and proud and disdainful toward those lower than ourselves. We feel happy when praised and upset when criticized. Like an unbridled horse, our disturbing emotions run out of control, all because of our self-centered attitude.

We are so self-centered that finding rat droppings on our pillow, we worry that a rat will nibble our ears. Hearing a clap of thunder, we worry that lightning will strike us on the head. In a haunted place our first worry is that we will be seized by the evil spirits who dwell there. Self-centeredness is the source of our fear. Some people suffer because they do not want to hear bad news, others suffer because they are unable to restrain their enemies or sustain their relatives. In all these cases selfishness is the source of all blame.

All our misfortunes arise because of our undisciplined mind. The mind is unruly due to our self-centered attitude. It is like aconite, the source of poison. It generates a host of emotions like hope and anxiety, and due to these we constantly face failure and calamity. Normally we point the finger at others, blaming them for whatever goes wrong. But the real root of problem, source of all trouble, the origin of all inauspiciousness and bad omens is the self-centered attitude that resides undisturbed at our heart. Throughout beginningless time we have loyally followed its leadership. So we should blame all our faults on it.

In order to transform our minds, we should follow the practical example of the great Kadampa masters. While chopping his brick-tea, one geshe would say to himself, "May I gain victory over the self-centered attitude," and imagine he was chopping it up too. Another would say, "I will stand guard at the doorway of my mind armed with the sharp spear of mindfulness. If self-centeredness attacks, I will attack. If he relaxes, I will relax, too."

Geshe Lang-ri Tang-pa would say, " 'Give profit and victory to sentient beings.' Why? Because all excellent qualities and happiness arise in dependence on them. 'Take all loss and defeat upon yourself.' Why? Because all suffering and harm come from holding yourself dear."

It is important to recognize the faults of our self-centered attitude and regard it as the enemy. You may be surrounded by failure and in the depths of misery. But if you know that the source of the calamity lies in your misconception of self and self-centered attitude, you will be aware that your prime task is to destroy them. Then unfavorable external factors will cease to have a hold on you, and the unceasing stream of fear, hope, and anxiety will settle down. Freed from them, you can relax.

Unless you are able to do such a practice, even should you become a monk or a nun wearing out a yak load of robes or having the initiation vase placed on your head a thousand times or spending your entire life listening to the Dharma, you will not become a practitioner of the Great Vehicle. But if you can apply what has been taught, you will become a follower of the Great Vehicle. Your mind will become expansive. You will be able to elevate others, and you will develop great wisdom.

If the Buddhas of the three times, the past, present, and future, were to explain for eons about the disadvantages and faults of the self-centered attitude and the disturbing emotions it gives rise to, there would be no end to it. However, the brief explanation we have just discussed is sufficient to make you aware of the faults of the self-centered attitude. It should inspire you to remove it.

Our past experiences, stimulated by external events, and our various plans for the future, have a common basis in the mind. The nature of the mind is mere clarity and awareness. Past experience is now merely an object of memory. Our future plans are only speculation. Such past and future events are just creations of the mind. Therefore, all our experiences, whether positive or negative, harmful or beneficial, are created by the mind. The Indian master Chandrakirti says,

The various worlds of sentient beings and
Their environments are created by the mind.
All sentient beings are produced by action,
But in the absence of mind, actions too do not
exist.

All our diverse experiences are manifestations of the mind. Depending on whether your mind is pacified or unruly, positive or negative, actions are committed. The internal environment, the individual's physical body, and the place where it abides, the external environment, arise through the force of action. The quality of that action depends on whether your mind is disciplined or not. Therefore, the myriad levels of happiness and suffering and the very structure of the environment depend heavily on whether your mind is tamed or untamed. This is why advice about disciplining the mind is so important.

In general, religion can be practiced physically and verbally. But the essential practice is to transform the mind. It means restraining the undisciplined, unpacified, and unruly mind from running amok. It means gradually transforming the mind that does not know how to cultivate the causes of happiness or eliminate suffering, even though that is what we desire.

The mind cannot be transformed by force, using knives and guns. It may seem to be weak, having no color or shape, but it is actually tough and resilient. The only way to change it is by using the mind itself. For only the mind can distinguish between what is to be done and what is to be given up. This is how the darkness of ignorance can be dispelled. When the mind can see the temporary and ultimate benefits of engaging in virtue and the faults of unvirtuous misdeeds, we will be able to act accordingly.

When we Buddhists take refuge in the Three Jewels, we tend to take refuge in someone else, the Buddha, and his qualities. But the actual refuge is the Dharma of true cessation and the true path that are to be attained by ourselves in the future. In order to achieve these qualities ourselves, at present we take refuge in someone who has already achieved the realization of knowledge and elimination of negativity. We seek knowledge from the Buddhas' experiences and ask them to guide us and shower upon us their blessings and protection. What is most important to understand is that your own future is in your own hands. As the Buddha has said, "I have shown you the path to nirvana, but nirvana is up to you."

In this context, blessing means improving our minds. When we ask someone to bless us, we are actually asking that person to help us improve our minds. Therefore, as religious practitioners the first and foremost thing we should remember is, "My practice is to discipline and transform my mind." Otherwise we might think that Dharma practice means performing rituals or playing drums and cymbals or merely reading the scriptures. These things are peripheral to the main practice, which is to alter or change the mind.

There are historical accounts of Kadampa masters meditating on the stages of the spiritual path. They would start by reciting their prayers in tune. Then they would remain completely silent in deep meditation as if they had fallen asleep. Similarly, acquaintances of the late Khun-nu Lama told me that whenever they went to see him they would usually find him with his upper robe over his head, deep in contemplation. They would not find him reciting prayers aloud. And yet when any-one approached him he would immediately uncover his head and ask what that person had come for.

People like this are the real practitioners. Instead of reciting prayers or mantras aloud they watch their minds. When the trend is positive, they rejoice and try to promote it, and when the trend is negative they apply antidotes. This is how they spend their time, watching the mind and sustaining uninterrupted mindfulness. Of course, it is initially very difficult. Some practition-ers of my acquaintance have told me that it is more dif-ficult to watch the mind than remain in a Chinese prison. This is their own personal experience. Meditat-ing one-pointedly, which means focusing all of one's mental attention on one object, without analyzing it, is very difficult. However, it is difficult in proportion to your degree of familiarity with it.

If you sustain your practice for a long time, it is def-inite that the mind will gradually develop. I am sure there are some among you who have that experience.

Most of us are still on an ordinary level of development. But if you compare your present behavior to your past behavior when you were not influenced by practice of the Dharma, you should notice some difference. I am certain that if we make an effort we can all improve our minds. The text says,

Meditate on the kindness of all sentient beings.

Sentient beings are extremely kind to us. The great Indian master Chandrakirti praised compassion as important in the beginning, middle, and end of our practice. This compassion is generated by reflecting on the helplessness and suffering of sentient beings. Compassion is the wish that sentient beings be free from the suffering. If sentient beings did not exist, we would have no basis for generating it.

The faults of our self-centered attitude and the benefits of concern for others are explained in the *Offering to the Spiritual Master:*

This chronic disease of self-centeredness
Is the cause of unwanted suffering.
Perceiving this, may I be inspired to blame,
    begrudge,
And destroy this monstrous demon of
    selfishness.

Caring for my mothers and seeking to secure them
    in bliss
Is the gateway to infinite virtue.

Seeing this, may I be inspired to hold them dearer
   than my life,
Even should they rise up as my enemies.

It is important to think again and again about the
benefits of concern for others and the faults of self-
centeredness. You can do so by reflecting on your own
personal experience, by observing others, and by reading. Two people may read the same book, but because
of differences in their attitudes they will each derive a
different meaning from what they read. An ordinary
person reading a story will tend to develop more attachment and hatred. A person with some experience of the
awakening mind will be able to see the story in terms of
the benefits of helping other people. And for someone
who has actually achieved some mental transformation,
whatever appears will become a teaching. For such a
person even day-to-day experience will be a source of
spiritual teachings. That is what is meant by being able
to see an instruction in everything visible.

There are many ways of contemplating the faults of
self-centeredness, the advantages of concern for others,
and the actual mind of exchanging oneself for others.
Again the *Offering to the Spiritual Master* explains it
succinctly:

In brief, the childish labor only for their own
   ends
While Buddhas work solely for others.
Understanding the distinctions between their
   respective faults and virtues,

> May I be inspired to be able to exchange myself
> for others.

The difference between childish, immature beings who are intent only on pursuing their own interests and fully awakened Buddhas who work only for the sake of others is easy to see. Ordinary childish beings like us are completely and willingly dominated by the self-centered attitude. The Buddhas, perceiving the faults of selfishness, voluntarily concern themselves with the welfare of the others. Exchanging yourself for the others does not mean merely thinking of others as yourself and yourself as others. It means taking your attitude of regarding yourself as very precious and applying it to others, regarding them instead as very precious. Your previous attitude of neglect, which is how you used to regard others, should now be applied to yourself.

This does not mean that you should not think about yourself at all. But in the context of fulfilling the purpose of others, you should neglect your own interests. If you have to choose between your own interests and the welfare of others, their interests come first. In short, if you put yourself at the disposal of others, you will find happiness in this life and in future lives, and finally you will achieve the state of omniscience. If you use others for your own personal ends, you will acquire many enemies and people will speak badly of you. Your pride will swell. When pride develops, jealousy grows. You become competitive, disdainful of others, and insolent toward superiors. Therefore, if you think highly of yourself and disregard others, even in this life you will encounter an unceasing host of calamities. When you come to die, everyone who knows you will rejoice saying, "It's good that this mean person is dead." Some people might even say that your death did not come soon enough.

On the other hand, if you make yourself available to others, regarding them as of primary importance and trying to help them by all possible means, everyone will regard you as a friend and hold you dear in their hearts. When we talk about others like this it does not necessarily mean all sentient beings, because we cannot actually relate to all sentient beings. What it does mean is that you should try as much as possible to help the sentient beings you live and associate with. If you then face difficulties, everyone will rush to help you. When you fall sick, people will come to look after you, even if they give you no more than a glass of water. Finally, on the day you die, everyone will feel the loss and say, "Alas, we lost a good friend, we're going to miss her." This will be your experience in this life. And in future lives, because you have accumulated merit by concerning yourself with others, your happiness will only increase.

Therefore, there is no need to cite scriptural quotations and evoke logical reasoning to substantiate the benefits of concern for others and the faults of self-centeredness. It is evident from our daily experience. We have obtained a human intelligence, and, whoever we are, we understand the importance of doing what is beneficial in the long run. Although for a beginningless time we have thought only of happiness and the avoidance of suffering, our present plight is plain for all to see. Regardless of whether we enjoy high or low status, whether we are rich or poor, we are daily confronted with a host of difficulties and misfortunes. Whenever we greet someone we ask after each other's health. The initial conversation will be pleasant and good, but if we have enough time to talk easily, inevitably complaints will creep in.

For time without measure we have selfishly cherished ourselves, but the way we have gone about it has been the stubborn way of the fool. Consequently, we achieved nothing we can now safely rely on. Now we have an opportunity to study these precious teachings and the potential to discriminate between what should be done and what should be dropped. We must recognize the self-centered attitude as our sworn enemy and not let ourselves be overpowered by it. We must wage war against it with all our strength. Recognizing concern for others as the source of all positive qualities, we must do whatever we can to cultivate it. So taking responsibility for the welfare of those you have previously neglected is called exchanging yourself for the others.

To increase fortitude, the practice of giving and taking is taught. By focusing on the practice of taking the sufferings of others onto yourself, you enhance compassion, and by focusing on the practice of giving others your happiness, you foster a sense of love. This is how the practice of giving and taking is related to meditation on love and compassion. According to some instructions the practice of taking is done first and the practice of giving is done second. Some instructions present it the other way around. Whichever way you do it, the practice of taking with compassion and the practice of giving with love give rise to the special resolve to free all beings from suffering, and that leads to the awakening mind.

Generating love and compassion is extremely important for your practice in the beginning, in the middle, and in the end when you attain Buddhahood. And it is only by attaining the fully awakened state of a Buddha that you have the capacity to fulfill the purposes of sentient beings. Practices like the four means of gathering disciples (giving, speaking pleasantly, teaching, and acting in accordance with the teachings) and the six perfections (generosity, discipline, patience, effort, concentration, and wisdom) are actually generated in dependence on sentient beings. All the fruitful practices of the Great Vehicle arise in relation to concern for the welfare of other sentient beings. Therefore, whenever your gaze falls upon a sentient being, thinking, "I shall fully awaken by depending on such beings as this," behold her with love and compassion.

Just as you will be able to harvest good crops if you plant healthy seeds in fertile soil, by cherishing sentient beings you will reap the fine crop of Buddhahood. By cherishing the welfare of sentient beings, you will be able to attain both good rebirth and the full awakening of a Buddha. The many types of suffering experienced by animals, hungry spirits, and the inhabitants of hell are the result of harming sentient beings. Neglecting the welfare of sentient beings, you will encounter the miseries of eating and being eaten by others, hunger and thirst and overwhelming and unrelenting pain.

Of course, some sentient beings might appear to be quite harmful to you. This is mainly the result of your own negative activities stimulated by disturbing emotions over many lives. Your having harmed other sentient beings in the past acts as an auxiliary condition. When the causes and conditions are activated and negative thoughts arise within the minds of other sentient beings, they harm you. However, those sentient beings who are harming you now have been your mother many times in previous lives. In other lifetimes, when they were reborn as animals, you have eaten their flesh, drunk their blood, gnawed their bones, used their skins, sucked their milk, and so forth. Therefore, if at this time you run into certain problems with these sentient beings, you should pay more attention to repaying the great kindness you have received from them in the past. Feel gratitude and love toward them, wishing that they be happy. Reflect that even when they harm you, they provide you with an opportunity to generate patience. This is an example of how to cultivate the practice of the six perfections in dependence on the kindness of sentient beings.

It is sentient beings who can place the state of Buddhahood in the palm of your hand. Whether someone is your enemy or your friend, if you are able to see those who are otherwise objects of disturbing emotions as your spiritual friends, you will be happy wherever you are. You regard as very kind the spiritual teacher who has given you teachings, which are a cause for liberation and enlightenment. Similarly, you should also remember the kindness of sentient beings who give you the chance to develop patience. To forget it is like being given delicious food and then spitting it out.

If you are able to practice in this way, then as the saying goes, "With courage you will be able to cross the plain of swords, because you will always find weapons at hand," or "Journeying to the treasure islands in search of jewels, you will discover jewels so abundant that you won't find a stone to ward off the dogs." There will be no time when you are not training the mind. You will regard nothing as an obstacle to your practice. You should cultivate the forbearance that is not discouraged when you are harmed or opposed. The more you are harmed, the more you should be able to develop patience and compassion toward whoever is harming you. If you are able to do that, even if you are besieged by antagonists, it will become a source of merit and compassion. This is the practice in which all teachings converge. Your practice will be like a panacea for all ailments. If you have such a practice of mind training it does not matter what you call it. The goddess Palden Lhamo has a hundred names and a thousand characteristics; whatever name you call her by is her name. This advice to transform misfortune into the path of enlightenment is again succinctly expressed in the *Offering to the Spiritual Master:*

> Though the world and its beings be full of the
>   fruits of misdeeds,
> And unwished-for sufferings pour upon me like
>   rain,
> Inspire me to see them as means to exhaust the
>   results of negative actions,
> And to take these miserable conditions as a path.

Wherever we live and whomever we associate with, we are always grumbling and pointing out what they have done wrong. As a result we are always unhappy. There is no need to elaborate the advantages of concern for the welfare of sentient beings and the disadvantages of the self-centeredness. There is no need to say more; simply look at the difference between ordinary immature people who work for their own benefit and the Buddha who works for the purpose of others.

There is a difference in the two approaches to cultivating concern for the welfare of other sentient beings. You can see sentient beings in a pleasing light by remembering their kindness to you over many lives. You respond to them because they have benefited you. However, this attitude borders on the opportunistic: "I'll take care of you because you have been kind to me, otherwise, why should I bother?" On the other hand, when you cultivate concern for the welfare of other sentient beings simply because they are like you in wanting happiness and not wanting suffering, you do not think about whether they have benefited you or not. You simply think that they have the same nature of wanting happiness and not wanting suffering as you do and they have the same right to achieve happiness and dispel suffering. I think this train of thought will be more effective and more useful for some people. If you compare yourself with other sentient beings, even though you have a right to happiness, you are just one person, whereas other sentient beings are infinite. Not only is your own happiness and suffering related to others, but the more you help them, the happier you will be. The more you harm or neglect them, the more miserable you will be. Therefore, sacrificing your own interests for the sake of the majority is the more intelligent approach. This, briefly, is how to practice exchanging yourself for others.

We can take the practice of cultivating the awakening mind to heart by meditating first on love and then on compassion. The text says:

Practice a combination of giving and taking.

You meditate on love by meditating on giving your body, wealth, and positive qualities to other sentient beings. If we dedicate our body, wealth, and virtuous qualities to others, they will serve some purpose. If we hoard them and protect them for ourselves, they will only bring frustration. First, we have to reflect on the advantages of training the mind to generate love by giving these things away. One sutra says that even if you were to make offerings as extensive as the countless realms of the universe to countless supreme beings, the benefits that would accrue would not compare to those deriving from generating love for even a moment. Similarly, Nagarjuna says that the merit you accumulate by meditating on love for even a moment surpasses what you would earn by giving three hundred pots of food three times a day to those who are hungry.

Whenever we encounter sickness or some other cause of unhappiness, instead of meditating on love and compassion we Tibetans have a tendency to talk about being disturbed by evil spirits. This is a disgrace for Buddhist practitioners. We profess not to believe in external forces of creation. Yet, instead of thinking about the power of our own minds, always to point to negative forces as responsible for disturbing us is in itself a great disturbance. To say we do not believe in a creator god and at the same time to act as if all our successes were due to pleasing spirits and that all our sufferings are created by displeasing them is like diluting the Dharma. It may be that in a few cases our difficulties are the work of evil spirits. However, the main source of trouble is within ourselves. We have negative experiences because of our negative actions.

Sometimes when we think that negative forces or evil spirits are interfering with us we try to stop it by asking someone to perform a ritual. This is supposed to drive evil spirits away. But the real method for overcoming such problems is to engage in such practices as love and compassion. Sometimes if I discover that certain harmful spirits are at work, I deliberately meditate on love and compassion for them. I feel that this does help. Meditation on love and compassion is our best protection.

A bodhisattva who has gone into solitude to meditate draws his or her mind within and meditates from the depths of his or her heart on how to help other people. There are two aspects to this meditation: giving to sentient beings, who live in the world, and giving to the environment they inhabit. Of course, initially we may not be able actually to give our bodies away. We should not do so until our practice both of the method and wisdom is stable and profound. But if we do not familiarize ourselves with the idea, it will be difficult to develop the necessary courage to do so. Therefore, to begin with we can visualize giving our bodies away. How do we do this?

First of all, think about how all sentient beings are the same in wanting happiness and not wanting suffering, and how they are deprived of happiness. When you have a strong feeling of this within yourself, think how good it would be if you were capable of making them happy. From the depths of your heart, dedicate all your positive qualities, your physical, mental, and verbal qualities, your wealth, and whatever you have, to them with the wish that they meet with happiness and whatever they need. In your imagination transform your positive qualities according to the needs of different sentient beings, wherever they are, even inhabiting the eight hot hells or the eight cold hells. Then think that satisfying these beings' needs becomes a favorable condition for their entry into practice of the Great Vehicle.

When you meditate on giving your body to others, do not visualize it in the form of impure blood, flesh, and so forth. You should mentally transform your body into a wish-fulfilling jewel, then you can give it in whatever form will be useful to sentient beings. Visualize your body transformed into food for those famished by hunger. Visualize yourself as a protector for those without protection or as a guide for those on an unfamiliar road.

In the same way, visualize giving others the internal conditions necessary for practicing the path, such as faith, diligence, concentration, and wisdom. After preparing the internal facilities and conditions, imagine giving them the external conditions for practice, such as a fully qualified teacher of the Great Vehicle and scriptures. You should imagine that all sentient beings' immediate wishes are fulfilled. As a result they are able to overcome the force of their disturbing emotions. In short, you should think that they are able to generate love and compassion, the root of the awakening mind. They can engage in the practice of the six perfections: generosity, ethics, patience, effort, meditation, and wisdom. They can gather the two accumulations of merit and insight and so attain the fully awakened state of a Buddha. As you complete the visualization of each round of giving, develop a deep sense of joy.

You can also visualize giving your transformed body to sentient beings experiencing specific sufferings in ways that will relieve them. To inhabitants of the hot hells you should imagine giving relief from their sufferings of heat. Similarly, as hungry spirits are overwhelmed by hunger and thirst, you should imagine first removing their immediate fear of not finding enough to eat. Then imagine gradually leading them onto the path of enlightenment. In this way you can think about first alleviating the specific sufferings of sentient beings in each of the six realms of existence (gods, demigods, humans, animals, hungry ghosts, and hell beings). Then gradually lead them onto the spiritual path and cause them to attain the fully awakened state of a Buddha.

By force of your awakening mind and the power of truth, invite into your presence all those who do you harm. Tell them that over beginningless time they have been your mother many times and at those times have benefited you and have protected you from many sufferings. Tell them it is now your responsibility to repay them, and ask them to take whatever they desire, whether it is your flesh, blood, bones, or skin. Develop a strong sense of compassion for them and give them these things. Recollect their great kindness and recall whatever debts you owe them, thinking that the time has now come to repay them. Provide those who seek shelter, food, wealth, and clothing with whatever they wish, requesting them to partake of it at their leisure. Imagine that they enjoy what you give them, that it fulfills their wishes, and that at the end they are satisfied. Imagine that this pacifies their harmful intentions and makes their minds receptive for the practice of Dharma, eventually leading them to enjoy the bliss of enlightenment. Although sentient beings desire happiness and wish to avoid suffering, they do not know how to fulfill their wishes properly. Imagine that by transforming your body, wealth, and so forth, you give them what they seek as well as guidance about how to find it themselves.

The second group of sentient beings to whom you can give your body are those who have entered the path. Think about helping those sentient beings who aspire for liberation to meet with the necessary external and internal facilities. Imagine that you transform your body into factors that would inspire them to enter the path of the Great Vehicle, which culminates in the achievement of Buddhahood. Then offer your body to the lineage of spiritual teachers and the Buddhas abiding in the ten directions (north, east, south, west, northeast, northwest, southeast, southwest, up, and down). You can visualize your body replicated as countless burning butter lamps or visualize countless emanations of your body making prostrations. In this way you can make countless numbers of offerings to the holy objects of refuge.

Next is the practice of giving to the environment. Again think about your body being transformed into a wish-granting jewel that can free the whole environment from negative features, such as barren land, thorny bushes, and stony ground. The whole environment becomes purified and pleasant. Even the sound

of the breeze in the trees inspires sentient beings to engage in the practice of Dharma. When you come to the
practice of giving away your wealth and belongings,
imagine transforming them too into objects to satisfy
other sentient beings. When they are received they will
serve as conditions for inspiring sentient beings to engage in the practice of the Dharma.

Next is the meditation on giving away your virtues.
Unlike the previous round of offerings, giving away
objects that you presently possess, you can dedicate to
others the virtue that you have created, are creating,
and will create. You should recall the virtuous deeds of
your body, speech, and mind, from simple things like a
gift of food to an animal up to the generation of the
awakening mind, with joyful admiration. Visualize
giving them all to sentient beings. It is very important
first to generate great love and concern for other sentient beings. Contrary to their desire for leisure and
happiness, they are in pain and distress, oppressed by
suffering and its causes. Imagine relieving all beings in
all worlds of their misery by the gift of your virtues.
Think that they each acquire the complete causes and
conditions for awakening to enlightenment.

Such meditation on generosity may not immediately help others in practical terms, but its value is not
to be underestimated. By means of such practices, we
develop the courage to be truly generous. The significance of training our minds in giving in this way is that
we will release ourselves from the grip of miserliness.
At present we might not be able to work practically for

the welfare of others, but it is very important to train ourselves in a generous attitude. By doing so on an imaginary level, we create a familiarity with giving. A time will come when we will have no hesitation in actually giving.

The more you think about something, the better your mind becomes acquainted with it. The time will come when your mind automatically flows in that direction. Even though you may not have the ability to benefit other people right now, you must prepare your mind to do so. Whoever has such a thought will eventually put it into actual practice. Mentally rehearsing these virtuous practices and rejoicing in them will lead to your gradually engaging in the actual practice of giving. What is the benefit of such visualization? If you have a direct karmic connection with another person, then even your visualization can help that person. Those with whom you have no special karmic connection may not receive much direct benefit, but you will be able to strengthen your mind in such a practice.

Now that you have visualized giving away your body, wealth, and spiritual qualities and dedicated them all to other sentient beings, can you continue to use them? Since you have sincerely dedicated your wealth and so forth to others, when you make use of them yourself, you should do so not in a selfish, possessive way but in order to benefit others. You should think that just as you have put your body and all these material facilities at other beings' disposal, even your own survival is for their benefit. There is nothing wrong with making use of your wealth, if you do so with a proper mental attitude. You may worry that you are merely dedicating these things to others in your imagination while you actually keep them for yourself. You may ask, What is the significance of dedicating them to others? The significance is in releasing the mind from the grip of miserliness, which is a product of the self-centered attitude.

The practices of giving and taking are complementary. We need to put them into practice alternately. To motivate ourselves, we should think about the plight of suffering beings on the one hand and the benefits of compassion on the other. Sentient beings are under the influence of disturbing emotions like ignorance, desire, animosity, and jealousy. Consequently, they cannot enjoy the happiness they wish for but constantly suffer varieties of pain. Compassion is the source of the awakening mind, which activates other meritorious deeds.

The Buddha said that bodhisattvas may not be able to engage in many practices but should cherish one quality. And if they have that one quality, it is equal to having all the qualities of the Buddha in the palm of the hand. What is that quality? It is great compassion. Wherever great compassion exists, there is the Buddha's doctrine. When a bodhisattva has great compassion, all other noble qualities will be present. It is like the faculty of life, from whose presence the sense faculties arise. Training in compassion is as good as practicing the entire range of the Buddha's teachings. The great Indian scholar Chandrakirti praised it as the seed at the beginning, the moisture in the middle, and the actual ripening of the fruit of enlightenment in the end.

We naturally have the potential for compassion within us. This is why we spontaneously react when we see someone wracked with pain. We all have a germ of kindheartedness. What we have to do is explore and develop this faculty within us. To do so we must overcome the anger and hatred that are products of our self-centered attitude. Therefore, it is the practice of bodhisattvas to attend to other beings' welfare before their own. If you adopt that kind of attitude, although your compassion and kindness may be very weak to begin with, they can be developed to an infinite degree. The primary aim of the practice of taking on sufferings is to eliminate the self-centered attitude. If you apply this practice with dedication, you will find it effective. The practice of taking on suffering is one of the most forceful techniques for controlling self-centeredness.

In generating compassion you should think about the sufferings of other sentient beings and reflect that when it comes to yourself, you are hardly able to tolerate even the slightest suffering. Sentient beings do not want suffering but do not know how to overcome it because of ignorance. The only way to help them is to generate the special mental attitude of taking responsibility from the depths of your heart to remove their suffering. You should not do this thinking, "If I implement the practice of giving and taking, I will ultimately benefit." That is the wrong motivation. You should think about the sufferings of other sentient beings and generate an intention to take on those sufferings. And when you think about your positive qualities, you should try to give or share them with other sentient beings.

Without such a pure altruistic motivation you might pursue the practice of giving and taking as a kind of daily practice and come to think of it as a source of your own benefit. If you do this, your practice will not be successful. On the other hand, if you think about helping other sentient beings and take on their suffering, whatever hardships you encounter will make your practice more effective. Taking on the sufferings of other sentient beings means we should think of taking on their self-centered attitudes, their sicknesses, and the causes of their sickness. You receive all these sufferings at the core of your heart.

Similarly, when you see a blind person or someone who has lost a limb, at least visualize giving that person one of your own eyes or one of your limbs. Doing this meditation sincerely will definitely reduce your self-centered attitude and enhance your practice of giving and taking.

The text says:

Giving and taking should be practiced alternately
And you should begin by taking from yourself.

In order to familiarize your mind with the practice of taking on suffering gradually, you should start with your own. First you should think about taking on and accepting all the sufferings you are to undergo in the future. You take them on now. Imagine taking on in this present life the sufferings you are to undergo in future lives. Then imagine taking on in this year the sufferings you are to undergo in the rest of your life. Imagine taking on today the sufferings you are to undergo in the rest of this year. You should imagine taking on not only the sufferings themselves, but even the causes and conditions that are responsible for them—delusion and disturbing emotions. Then imagine taking on sufferings of other sentient beings along with their causes and conditions.

Taking on others' sufferings does not mean that you go through this process of imagining and their sufferings simply disappear. Nor is it as if you receive their sufferings and just put them aside. You should think of taking their sufferings to the core of your heart. This has the special effect of striking at the self-centered attitude abiding there. Imagine that all the sufferings of other sentient beings with their causes and conditions are removed from them just like clumps of dark hair shaved off with a sharp razor. Then imagine taking all these dark clumps of suffering into your heart. Think that all sentient beings are freed from sufferings along with the causes and conditions of their sufferings.

In order to improve the effectiveness of your meditation it is wise to meditate on specific individuals and realms instead of all sentient beings in general. You can visualize taking on the sufferings and their causes of the beings in celestial worlds, then those of the human world. Continue the meditation by taking on the misery with its causes of those in the animal, the hungry spirit, and hell worlds. There are no rigid rules with regard to the object of your meditation. You are at liberty to vary it according to your taste and spiritual development. At times you can visualize taking on the miseries and their causes of the beings in all the realms of existence in one meditation session. At other times you may like to meditate on taking on the sufferings of one specific world for weeks and months. You can also imagine taking on the sufferings of beings who have entered the spiritual path. Even bodhisattvas who have attained the tenth spiritual level have imprints of the misconception of self still to be removed. Of course, the Buddhas have no sufferings to be taken on. Nor is there anything you can take on from your spiritual master.

In any case, the purpose of the entire meditation is to reduce and eliminate the self-centered attitude and promote and enhance your thoughts of concern for other sentient beings. The practice must come from the core of your heart. It should not be polluted by self-interest, thinking that this virtuous action will bring you peace, happiness, and a long life. What is meant here by concern for others is holding them dear not out of attachment, but through clear realization of their importance. Ultimately all sentient beings can attain the fully awakened state of a Buddha, because every being possesses the intrinsic Buddha nature. You apply the way you would normally think of yourself to others.

The visualization of giving and taking should be done vigorously so that it will have some effect on our instinctively selfish attitude. Eventually we come to feel a strong aversion for our self-centeredness. Once our love for others is strongly developed, we will spontaneously ask ourselves what we do for others. Whether or not our working for other sentient beings actually brings them closer to enlightenment, such a visualization really helps strengthen our compassion and love. This is done in conjunction with the process of breathing. As the text says,

These two should be made to ride on the breath.

As you exhale, visualize giving your body, possessions, and virtues of the three times (past, present, and future) to sentient beings as limitless as space. Imagine that they obtain uncontaminated bliss. As you inhale, visualize taking the sufferings and faults of other sentient beings, as well as their causes, into the core of your heart. Imagine that they become completely free from misery and its causes. If you are able to train in this way, since the mind and breath will flow in the same direction, you will overcome distraction and strengthen mindfulness. This will have a positive effect on your meditation. What is more, even the ordinary action of breathing will become a factor in your working for the welfare of other sentient beings.

Our endeavors should not be confined only to meditation sessions. We must be equally alert and conscientious during the postmeditation period. Whatever spiritual insights we gain during meditation must prove their value during the postmeditation period. Similarly, whatever understanding is gained during this period should promote and enhance our meditation. It is common for people to be serious during their meditation but to suffer a kind of laxity after the session, indulging in undisciplined actions of body, speech, and mind. We need to make sure that we do not fall into this trap. It is extremely important to watch the state of our minds. The text says,

> Concerning the three objects, three poisons, and
>   three virtues,
> The instruction to be followed, in brief,
> Is to take these words to heart in all activities.

The mind has the potential to create all kinds of negative thoughts and emotions when it comes into contact with objects of the senses. When you meet or think about someone who annoys you, anger and hostility arise. When you come across something you want, desire arises. Under such circumstances, you must not allow these disturbing emotions to overpower you. This is a time to take advantage of them to strengthen your mind training. You should generate compassion for all sentient beings who are similarly afflicted. Think about the defects of disturbing emotions and the unpleasant consequences they produce. Make a wish that by your experience of anger, for example, all other sentient beings may be free of anger and may avoid the suffering that is its consequence. You can think along the same lines when you experience attachment, ignorance, and so forth. At the end, think that all beings enjoy peace and bliss. Generally, bodhisattvas try to prevent disturbing emotions arising. When they arise naturally, instead of becoming depressed, they rationalize and pray that all other sentient beings may not have to suffer the same way. Whatever you are doing during the post-meditation period, whether you are working, eating, sitting, or walking, you must be alert and aware.

Especially if you follow an active life in society, when faced with different situations you should not let yourself become a victim of circumstances. Instead, you should transform adverse circumstances into factors for training the mind. In order to remind yourself of this it may be helpful to recite certain verses to yourself, such as:

> May their misdeeds ripen on me
> And may all my virtues ripen on them.
> May all sentient beings' sufferings mature on me
> And through my virtues may they all be happy.
> Whatever agonies beings may suffer
> May they ripen on me alone.
> Through all the virtues of bodhisattvas
> May wandering beings enjoy bliss.

Giving and taking is a practice that should be undertaken with great mental courage and determination. The great Sha-ra-wa said that if you really want to accustom your mind to such an instruction, your practice should not be merely like a stone tumbling down a steep slope, nor should it be like lukewarm water in a stagnant pool. It should be red as blood and white as curd. This means that to train your mind you should not be halfhearted, hesitant, or apprehensive but totally dedicated and decisive. You should know the difference between black and white. You cannot expect to engage in the practice of mind training one day and the next day do something else if you are looking for success.

Having trained in love and compassion, you might wonder why you need to attain the fully awakened state of a Buddha. The great beings intent on personal liberation and bodhisattvas on the tenth level of spiritual development have a great capacity to help other beings. However, only by attaining complete enlightenment can they place innumerable beings in the state beyond suffering. Therefore, you should generate a strong aspiration to attain the fully awakened state of a Buddha capable of fulfilling both your own and others' purposes.

Nowadays, many of us might doubt whether it is really possible to reach the state of Buddhahood. When we talk about Buddhahood we might think only of Buddha Shakyamuni, who appeared in this world just over 2,500 years ago. Therefore, it is important to have a good understanding of the nature of enlightenment. First we have to understand the possibility of removing the faults that contaminate our minds. This is what makes the attainment of enlightenment possible. If we can understand that, it will inspire our efforts to generate the awakening mind. Therefore, it is said that wisdom focuses on enlightenment and compassion focuses on the needs of other sentient beings. Once we appreciate the possibility of attaining enlightenment within our own minds, we will aspire to achieve it.

CHAPTER 6

CALLING THE AWAKENED

TO WITNESS

*At this point let us formally generate
the precious awakening mind.
This will require that we remain alert,*

recite the prayers, and follow the visualizations carefully.

The supreme practice of the Dharma is the practice of the Great Vehicle. Fundamental to the Great Vehicle is the development of the awakening mind, which has greater concern for others than for oneself. The awakening mind is the source of all good things. All temporary and ultimate happiness arises spontaneously and effortlessly in dependence on this mind. Even the slightest concern for others is a cause of happiness and puts others at ease. On the other hand, if, in pursuit of our own happiness, we disregard the welfare of others and are bent on harming them, it will have negative consequences in the long term as well as in the short term. We will find ourselves isolated and friendless, with no one to trust and confide in.

As intelligent human beings, we have the ability to discriminate between temporary and ultimate benefit. We are capable of setting aside lesser purposes in order to achieve a greater one. If we lack discrimination we will become engrossed in things of only superficial value and will be unable to plan and think beyond that. Since we possess this discrimination through the power of human intelligence, if we have to undergo certain problems in the short term in order to achieve a more lasting happiness, we will readily do so. From the greater perspective of human discrimination we will be prepared to forgo lesser gains for more significant purposes. As the Tibetan proverb has it: "Destroy one hundred and invite one thousand."

Now that we have obtained the potential of a human being, it is important to use it wisely. If we employ our discriminating intelligence only to disturb and upset others, we are wasting our human life. In that case it would definitely have been better not to have obtained it. Since we have at present found this precious life as a free and fortunate human being, the best we can do is to work for definite goodness in the future. Even if we are unable to do that, it is important to complete this life in a positive way. First, we should understand the positive qualities of the practice. Second, if we listen to or read the stories of exemplary figures of the past, we will have some model to follow, which will give us enthusiasm.

In his previous lives on the path, the Buddha was an ordinary individual like us. But due to the power of his awakening mind, his greater concern for others than himself, he never allowed himself to be carried away by disturbing emotions and negative actions. He performed only beneficial deeds. He engaged in the difficult practices of a bodhisattva from life to life over many eons. As a result he finally achieved the fully awakened state of a Buddha—the state completely free of faults and possessing all qualities. That is why we now regard him as the foremost object of refuge, referring to him as the omniscient teacher.

The compassionate Buddha was able to become enlightened because the essence of even the contaminated mind is emptiness, the ultimate reality. It is because of this that faults can be eliminated, qualities can be cultivated, and the omniscient mind can be attained. Likewise, we too can make the attempt. If we rely on a continuous practice of virtue like the uninterrupted flow of water, we have the natural resources to improve from life to life. The ultimate essence is within us by nature, and we do not have to cultivate it afresh, as is stated in Maitreya's *Ornament of Realization:*

> Since the Buddha's body is radiant,
> Since there is no difference in the reality,
> Since all possess the lineage,
> All embodied beings possess the Buddha essence.

So, keeping the experience of our teacher in mind, we should practice mainly cultivating the awakening mind, having more concern for others than ourselves. In our day-to-day lives we should pay repeated attention to the instructions for training in the awakening mind by frequently reciting the following verse:

I take refuge in the Buddha, Dharma, and spiritual
community,
Until I attain the state of enlightenment.
By the force of generosity and other virtues,
May I achieve Buddhahood to benefit all sentient
beings.

This is extremely important for developing a positive attitude and avoiding being overwhelmed by hostile forces. The more we generate such an attitude and
the more we make our minds familiar with positive
qualities and appreciate their benefits, the more stable
and more incorruptible our minds will become. Without such a practice, we may be able to generate a positive mind to some extent. However, if we do not constantly familiarize ourselves with it, it will become like
weak tea. This is only natural.

The scriptures describe twenty-two kinds of awakening mind. It is said that until you have attained the
stability of the earthlike awakening mind or the gold-
like awakening mind, there is a risk of your awakening
mind degenerating. For this reason it is important that
development of the qualities of compassion should be
augmented by wisdom, and development of the qualities of wisdom should be augmented by compassion.
Compassion and wisdom should be practiced in combination. Familiarity with the practice is a key factor.
And since many of us readily talk about "all mother
sentient beings" or "the sentient beings of the six realms
of existence," it is important to have some idea of what

the awakening mind is and to familiarize ourselves with it through repeated practice.

At this point we will recite the prayer for formally generating the aspirational awakening mind. If you have a painting of the Buddha, visualize it as actually being the skillful and compassionate Buddha. Do not think that there is just a painted image before you, but imagine that the Buddha himself, who is motivated by compassion and who is the embodiment of compassion, and who is adorned with the major and the minor signs of a fully awakened being, is actually present. Around him visualize bodhisattvas who appear in celestial forms and likewise those who appear in human form, such as the great Indian teachers Asanga and Nagarjuna. Visualize all the exalted translators and scholars of ancient Buddhist India.

From Tibet, the Land of Snow, visualize the presence of great teachers from the period of the ancient translations, such as the abbot Shantarakshita and the master Padmasambhava and his twenty-five disciples. Likewise, from the period of the new transmission visualize the teachers of the major schools and lineages. In short, visualize all the exalted beings and bodhisattvas of the four traditions of Tibetan Buddhism, whether they are from Sakya, Geluk, Kagyu, or Nyingma. Visualize them all here in front of you as witnesses to your generation of the awakening mind.

The actual presence of these beings is a real possibility because they have all generated the awakening mind with greater concern for others than themselves.

They have trained in the difficult conduct of the bodhisattvas and striven for enlightenment. Since they have generated the awakening mind in the interest of all sentient beings, they have generated it on our behalf as well. Therefore, if on our part we look toward these beings as positive examples and we aim our minds in a positive direction, we will naturally receive their compassionate blessings spontaneously.

Visualize the Buddhas and bodhisattvas of the ten directions present in front of you. Around you visualize the infinite sentient beings of the six realms of existence. Think of these sentient beings who have been your mothers as being similar to yourself in wanting happiness and not wanting suffering. Even though they want happiness, they are deprived of it. And even though they do not want suffering, they are afflicted by it. This is how they are similar to you. What then is the difference? However pitiable we may be, we at least know that unwanted sufferings are the result of negative deeds. We know that despite the variety of these negative deeds, they are all due to our unpacified and undisciplined minds.

The principal cause of our minds' being obstructed and unruly is our misconception of true existence, the root of delusion. Our misconception is a temporary phenomenon, not validly established; therefore, it can be eliminated. If we think about this, we can identify the cause of suffering. Having found the cause of suffering, we can conclude that it too can be eliminated. This kind of understanding, whether we have confirmed it or not, changes our perspective on the future course of our lives.

Having generated the noble wish to benefit limitless sentient beings, we must work quickly to fulfill their temporary and ultimate aims. For this reason we need to attain the fully awakened state of a Buddha. Therefore, we must aspire to attain that unsurpassable state of perfection and purification for the sake of all mother sentient beings. Consequently, we undertake accumulating the necessary merit and generating such a mind in the presence of the Buddhas and the bodhisattvas assembled before us.

First, generate a strong sense of love and compassion for the sentient beings you have visualized around you. Then think, "To fulfill their great purpose I will generate the awakening mind, and to do that I will generate merit by means of the seven-branch ritual, taking the Buddhas and the bodhisattvas as my witness." Then, repeat this request for the awakening mind:

> Teacher, please listen to me. Just as those who have gone thus, those who have been liberated, the perfect and fully awakened Buddhas and the exalted bodhisattvas of the past have initially generated the unsurpassable, perfect, and complete awakening mind, similarly, O teacher, kindly help me by the name of _____ to generate the mind of unsurpassable, perfect, and complete awakening.

Here, and in the prayers below, say your own name in order to strengthen your sense of actually taking part. This completes the request. Next, we take refuge. Think about the Buddhas and the bodhisattvas you have already visualized in front of you. The Buddhas, who are the spiritual community of those who have completed the practice, and the bodhisattvas, the spiritual community of those still in training, represent our objects of refuge. What makes them so precious? It is the qualities they represent. And what are these qualities? The main one is the Dharma. The Dharma is the actual refuge that protects us from fear. Therefore, it is the Dharma, the true cessation and true path, within the minds of the Buddhas and bodhisattvas in front of you that represents the actual refuge. So, vividly recall the qualities of the Buddha, Dharma, and Sangha in front of you.

Now, what is the content of the request? The sentient beings that we have visualized around us desire happiness and do not want suffering. We all have an equal right to achieve happiness and remove suffering. But it is due to ignorance of what is to be practiced and what is to be given up that we are unable to put an end to suffering. Today, by the compassionate blessing of the Three Jewels, we have identified the naturally abiding factor that enables us to remove suffering and achieve happiness. Therefore, you should decide that you too will actualize the qualities of realization and abandonment possessed by the Buddhas and bodhisattvas.

The process of seeking refuge in the Three Jewels is not just a recitation of words. It is an aspiration to attain the same qualities of realization and abandonment as the Buddhas and the bodhisattvas in whom you presently take refuge. You should think that you are taking refuge so that you yourself and all other sentient beings attain the ranks of the jewel of the spiritual community by cultivating the Dharma of the true cessation and true path within you. And finally you will become a member of the spiritual community that is no longer training, a fully awakened Buddha.

Maintaining the entire visualization I have described, repeat the verse for taking refuge three times. If you are healthy you should kneel on your right knee, but if you are unwell or it is physically difficult for you, you can simply sit. As you visualize the Buddhas and the bodhisattvas as present before you, from the depths of your heart recall that they have generated the noble mind aspiring to awaken for all limitless sentient beings including yourself. Recall that their rope of compassion is extended to all sentient beings at all times. Think of these Buddhas and the bodhisattvas present before you as your object of refuge.

What is most important is to visualize all helpless sentient beings around you and to think that in order to liberate them from the suffering and its causes you must attain the state of a fully awakened Buddha. For that reason and with that motivation take refuge in the Buddhas and bodhisattvas while repeating this verse three times:

Teacher, kindly listen to me. I by the name _____ take refuge in the Buddha, supreme among human beings, from this time until I attain the essence of

enlightenment. O teacher, kindly listen to me.
I by the name _____ take refuge in the supreme
Dharma, the state of peace which is free of attachment, from this time until I attain the essence of
enlightenment. O teacher, kindly listen to me. I by
the name _____ take refuge in the supreme spiritual community, the exalted bodhisattvas of the
nonreturning stage, from this time until I attain
the essence of enlightenment.

If you seek only temporary protection there are
many other objects of refuge, but for those who aspire
to achieve liberation, the fully awakened Buddha,
the Dharma—his teaching and practice—and the
Sangha—the spiritual community—are the infallible
refuge.

Next we need to accumulate merit through the
seven-branch practice. The first of the seven branches
is bowing down as an act of respect. Prostrating yourself acts as an antidote to pride. Pride is the source of
many faults. We know that as human beings much depends on the way we think. Yet, from a certain perspective, in our thinking we seem to be inferior even to
insects. Insects have no idea what is to be practiced and
what is to be given up. They are not physically or mentally equipped to do so. On the other hand, we possess
discriminative awareness—we know what is to be
practiced and what is to be given up—and yet we
knowingly engage in improper activities. From that
angle we seem to be inferior even to insects.

Whenever I associate with others I will learn
To think of myself as the lowest amongst all
And respectfully hold others to be supreme
From the very depths of my heart.

This verse explains the kind of attitude we should cultivate in relation to others. Whatever the circumstances, we should remain humble. It is said that humility is the foundation for higher qualities. This is the start of real happiness. It is not helpful to be proud, thinking of ourselves as people who count. But we should differentiate between having low self-esteem, thinking of ourselves as worthless or incapable, and humility, which means being modest and without pride.

Low self-esteem, thinking that you cannot do anything, is something you should avoid in the context of both religious practice and worldly activities. A bodhisattva never submits to low self-esteem but with tremendous courage takes responsibility for fulfilling the welfare of all sentient beings. A bodhisattva has a healthy sense of confidence while having no pride at all. That is what we need. Paying respect by making prostrations acts as an antidote to pride. You can make prostrations physically, verbally, and mentally. Here, to prostrate means to bow down wholeheartedly and respectfully before the objects of refuge in thought, word, and deed.

The second branch, offering, is done to accumulate merit. You can either set up an actual arrangement of offerings or make mentally visualized offerings. If you have developed meditative stabilization and can maintain your concentration on the object, you can make mentally created offerings. Otherwise this option is not open to you. Through meditative stabilization you achieve what is called form through spiritual power. Even if you lack such power, you can mentally offer materials that are ownerless or belong to you.

The branch of confession is very important. Our minds have become contaminated and obstructed by our many past faults and misdeeds. The way to purify them involves nothing more than confession and restraint. Milarepa said, "If you are thinking of purifying your misdeeds, they can be purified by repentance." Misdeeds can be purified if you have a strong sense of remorse. Unvirtuous action can be purified if it is openly and regretfully admitted. Therefore, it is worth confessing misdeeds and refraining from their repetition.

The next branch entails rejoicing, which is a very skillful means of accumulating merit. If you rejoice in your virtuous activities, thinking of what you have done as meaningful and worth celebrating, its value is increased. If you do something virtuous and rejoice wholeheartedly without regret, its positive potential will be multiplied many times. This is an excellent way of enhancing your collection of virtue. Likewise, with regard to other people's virtuous activities, instead of feeling jealous or competitive about them, it is better to be admiring and rejoice from the depth of your heart. That way you will participate in the original virtue and accumulate merit.

Rejoicing at others' virtue includes not only the virtuous actions of other people but also the virtuous actions done by bodhisattvas and beings seeking personal liberation. It can also include admiring the qualities of the body, speech, and mind of the Buddhas. This is a practice with very extensive potential. Simply by rejoicing, you can accumulate great merit in a short time. On the negative side, it is also true that even a brief moment's anger or hatred can propel us into miserable states of existence for eons.

The next branch is to request awakened beings to turn the wheel of doctrine. From the depth of your heart, request the Buddhas and bodhisattvas you have visualized before you to teach. You request them to teach the Dharma continuously to sentient beings, including yourself, who are helpless, unprotected, and lacking discrimination between right and wrong.

Following that is the request to the Buddhas not to pass away. When the Buddha appears among us as a human being who takes birth, performs activities, and finally passes away, he is referred to as an emanation body. This is a request, therefore, that the Buddhas remain among us and do not pass away.

The final branch of dedication involves taking steps to prevent the fruit of our virtuous deeds from being carelessly wasted. We do this by dedicating it to the benefit and welfare of all sentient beings. We make the wish that by the power of the merit we have created we may attain Buddhahood on their behalf. We also pray that the Dharma may flourish both as scripture and inner realization. The substance to be dedicated in the practice of dedication is the merit and virtue we have created. Merely asking for something good to happen without having anything to dedicate would only be an aspirational prayer.

So, while visualizing the Buddhas and the bodhisattvas clearly in front of you as before, focus again on the sentient beings around you and generate intense feelings of love and compassion for them. Then reflect on the meaning of the seven branches of the practice.

Now we come to the actual formal generation of the awakening mind. To accomplish this and make a commitment, we first need to create some feeling for what we are doing. Merely reciting the words is not enough. Generating the awakening mind here refers to generating the altruistic aspiration for supreme enlightenment. Generation of the actual awakening mind comes about only after years of practice and in some cases might take several lives. This is because the genuine awakening mind is produced only after acquiring prolonged familiarity through meditation.

Nevertheless, what we can do now is to develop some understanding of the awakening mind and begin to familiarize ourselves with it. And what is the awakening mind? As we have already discussed, it is a mind focusing specifically on other sentient beings in a spirit of wishing to fulfill their ambitions. That leads to a wish to achieve enlightenment. Thus the aspiration to fulfill others' ambitions acts as the cause, and the aspiration for enlightenment assists it. So the awakening mind embodies these two aspirations.

If you think about the sentient beings you have visualized around you, all have an innate feeling of "I." Consequently, all of them naturally want this "I" to experience happiness and not suffering. In this, all of them are the same, even the tiniest insects. Religious practice, too, is based on this fundamental feeling. Such an attitude—wanting happiness and not wanting suffering—is quite reasonable. Our very existence is aimed at finding happiness. The purpose of human life is the achievement of happiness. In this context, Buddhahood is the ultimate state of happiness, it is the state of lasting happiness, it is the fulfillment of your own and others' purposes. In other words, Buddhahood is the best of everything.

We all want happiness and have a right to achieve it. Therefore, we all have a right to lasting happiness, success, and the best of everything. But, although this is what we want, we are ignorant of the causes of happiness. And although we do not want suffering, we are ignorant of what causes that, too. So, suffering is like a self-inflicted problem. Today we have found life as free and fortunate human beings and have met with the Buddha's teaching and practice. In particular, we have gained some acquaintance with the teachings of the Great Vehicle. So it is extremely important to look at things from a wider perspective, a profounder angle, and not be mistaken in our way of thinking.

If we pay careful attention, one factor of our predicament is that whoever we are, we neglect others and cherish ourselves. When you are concerned only with yourself, you have to spend your life in the worst situations. You will be reborn in miserable conditions. Even if you are reborn as a human being, your life will be short and you will frequently be sick and the butt of constant criticism and abuse. All such misfortunes arise from self-centeredly neglecting others.

If you reduce the tenacity of your self-centered attitude and strengthen your concern for others, trying to help them as much as you can, you will be happier, have more friends, and be free from regret. Therefore, concern for others is the root of all happiness, while self-centeredness leads to destruction. Misery, fear, and nightmares are all due to self-centeredness. When you are concerned for others there is no reason to be afraid. Even among those who have no interest in spiritual development, the more an individual cultivates a positive mind and a sense of universal responsibility, the happier she will be. Such a person will have greater access to comfortable facilities. People will more readily offer her assistance.

As human beings it is essential to have close friends, people who really care and show concern for you. Our ability to smile is a unique human feature. If you smile it makes others happy, and likewise it makes you happy if others smile at you. On the other hand, nobody likes a scowling face. That is human nature. Of course, sometimes deceitfulness and lies can be disguised by a grin. But if you smile sincerely, everyone will be pleased. This shows our innate delight in friendship. It is human nature to live in friendship and harmony. Then our lives will be meaningful and happy.

If we remain suspicious and full of ill feeling for each other, how are we to be happy? In order to create an amicable, harmonious atmosphere, we first have to cultivate an altruistic attitude from within. When we have that, friends will automatically gather around us. We will naturally find people on whom we can rely. It is a mistake to foster ill will, jealousy, competitiveness, and pride, lurking like a poisonous snake, making no effort to improve our attitude. If we expect change to come only from the outside without bringing about any mental transformation within, we will be disappointed. How can there be a result without a cause?

Therefore, from both a short- and long-term perspective, to be a good, warmhearted person is definitely the root of peace, happiness, and everything good. We do not have to cite quotations from scripture to prove this. This is our actual lived experience. If we look back on our lives, the only meaningful things we have done have been those activities intended to benefit others. It is difficult to assess how much benefit we have achieved even when trying to fulfill our own interests. Anyway, such benefits are now like last night's dreams, leaving little of practical value. What we are still carrying on our backs is the heavy burden of misdeeds, dishonesty, and deception.

If you have achieved some benefit and done some good, that is a cause for rejoicing. Looking back you will see that it was doing something directly or indirectly beneficial to others that made your life meaningful. What else in the many years that have elapsed would make you think you have led a meaningful life? So as you reflect on your past experiences, it is now important to determine that for the rest of your life, however long it may be, you will do only what brings joy and satisfaction. For my part, the things that I can now rejoice in are my determined spirit for the cause of Tibet and my generation of the wish to benefit all sentient beings. These are what have made my life meaningful, whether I was living in Tibet or India.

Trying to benefit others, directly or indirectly, using the full potential of your body, speech, and mind, is what makes your life meaningful. Therefore, even if you are unable to achieve any benefit yet, at least keep up the effort. It is even worth imagining that you are performing beneficial activities. Normally we only fantasize about doing something negative. That is silly and foolish. The Kadampa masters used to advise that with regard to doing something good, "Even if you have no teeth, chew with your gums." Now is the time for us to be alert and attentive.

Think of all the sentient beings around you as being like yourself in wanting happiness and not wanting suffering and as possessing equal potential to become Buddhas. Think to yourself, "Now I must do something for them. But when it comes to providing practical help, it is difficult at present for me to help even one sentient being completely. Therefore, may I attain the fully awakened state of a Buddha without delay for these sentient beings who have been my mothers. That is what I will definitely work for." This is the kind of determined attitude you should cultivate here. This is what is known as generating the awakening mind.

Let me summarize this again. Reflect deeply on the advantages of concern for others' welfare and the disadvantages of self-centeredness. Recalling your own past experience, confirm that the activities of body, speech, and mind based on self-centeredness lead nowhere, whereas activities that are the result of concern for other people are reliable and meaningful in the long run. Take refuge in the Buddhas and bodhisattvas visualized before you.

If you really trust the Buddha and take refuge from the depth of your heart, you must also consider how the Buddha feels. For example, on an everyday level if you like to do something that your close friend dislikes, you will try not to do it out of consideration for her. If you invite a friend to dinner who does not like hot or spicy food but you do, to add a lot of chili without consideration of your friend's taste would be a mistake. At least on that occasion it would be better to be more careful. So even in ordinary circumstances you take your friend's wishes into account. To do so indicates that you are her true friend. Therefore, since the

Buddha is someone to whom we have entrusted our long-term happiness, it is important to pay some attention to his intentions.

The Buddhas and the bodhisattvas show the same concern toward sentient beings that a mother shows her only child. So to neglect sentient beings even indirectly is to disregard the thoughts of the Buddha. It is contradictory to take refuge in the Buddhas and bodhisattvas and then on the practical level to neglect the welfare of the infinite, helpless sentient beings, on behalf of whom you have generated the awakening mind and attained enlightenment. If we are really unable to benefit them, at least we should avoid harming them.

In order formally to generate the awakening mind, please kneel as before, repeat the words, and generate the mind yourself. As I have explained, take the awakened Buddhas and bodhisattvas and the infinite sentient beings you have visualized as your witnesses. Resolve to actualize qualities like those of the Buddha's body, speech, and mind yourself. Then, as you focus on that intention, resolve never to give up that awakening mind you have generated, and repeat these words three times:

O Buddhas and bodhisattvas of the ten directions, please listen to me. O teacher, please listen to me. I by the name _____ have in this and other lives planted seeds of virtue through my own practice of generosity, ethics, keeping the vows, and other virtues and, likewise, by asking others to do practice and rejoicing at their practice. May these root virtues become a cause to cultivate the awakening mind, just as in the past those who have gone to bliss, those who have been liberated, the perfectly, fully awakened Buddhas, the great bodhisattvas seated on the highest ground have generated the awakening mind.

I by the name _____ from now until the attainment of the essence of Buddhahood, in order to liberate those sentient beings who are not liberated, deliver those who are not delivered, give breath to the breathless and those who have not fully gone beyond suffering, will cultivate the aspiration to attain the unsurpassable, perfect, and complete enlightenment.

In the course of our practice of mind training we cultivate love, wishing that all sentient beings meet with happiness and compassion, wishing that all sentient beings be freed from all sufferings. These twin attitudes bring forth the special attitude that causes us to wish, "I myself will make them meet with happiness and separate from suffering." You should think, "I will generate the great resolve that has been generated by the bodhisattvas of the past." As you focus on the Buddhas and bodhisattvas, cultivate faith.

As you remember the qualities of the body, speech, and mind of the Buddhas and the bodhisattvas, think that you, too, will before long achieve a similar ability to work effortlessly and spontaneously for others. And on the basis of that thought, take refuge in the Buddhas and bodhisattvas. Therefore, again resolve to generate the awakening mind, which aspires to supreme enlightenment for the sake of all sentient beings. With such intense feeling, repeat the above lines for the second time.

Today we have found a human life and encountered the Buddha's teaching and practice. Having come upon such an excellent opportunity, we must try to extract the essence from it. The essence of Dharma practice is the awakening mind. We should reflect that to be able to generate such a mind even on an imaginary level is really fortunate. Generating the awakening mind is like an offering of practice to the Buddhas and bodhisattvas. It is the way to fulfill the temporary and permanent wishes of sentient beings. All welfare and happiness arise from this mind. The Buddhas and bodhisattvas of the past have also generated such a mind again and again and finally attained the fully awakened state of enlightenment. Having found this precious opportunity today, you should think, "I will also generate this mind as has been generated by the Buddhas and the bodhisattvas of the past." With intense feeling, repeat these lines of holding the awakening mind for the third time. And this time, reflect that self-centeredness is like a poisonous root and consideration for others is like a medicinal root, the source of the collection of virtue.

Since we have generated this aspiring awakening mind, we must observe certain practices to prevent this mind from degenerating. We should remember the beneficial qualities of this mind again and again. More important is never to give up the welfare of other sentient beings. In the future, whatever kinds of sentient beings we encounter, we should never wish for them to meet with misfortune.

Now, in the case of Tibetans, for example, it may seem that the Communist Chinese are the greatest obstacle to the flourishing of the Dharma. But it is improper to focus on that and wish disasters to befall the Chinese. We have taken a commitment to ensure the welfare of all sentient beings. If we exclude the welfare of the Chinese, we are shutting out a section of all sentient beings. This means we are breaking our earlier commitment to the welfare of all sentient beings.

This is not to say that we should surrender in the face of other people's negative activities. A number of people have told me that if I talk too much about spiritual practice we may never be able to fight back against the Chinese. Here we have to differentiate between romantic courage and true courage. In the context of generating the awakening mind, we are talking about real courage, real determination. There is no mental determination or courage stronger and purer than the awakening mind. So of course you can respond to other people's wrongs, but without letting compassion and love slip from your mind. In explaining the bodhisattva's conduct, permission is given to behave physically and verbally in ways that would otherwise seem to be negative if the action will actually benefit other people. When we talk about cultivating the bodhisattva's conduct, we are not turning ourselves into cowards.

As I have explained before, one of the best methods for preventing this mind from degenerating is to recite the verse for taking refuge and generating the awakening mind. In order to enhance your practice of the awakening mind, you should do this practice three times in the daytime and three times at night.

There are two ways to collect virtue. The collection of merit is acquired by generating compassion, love, and the awakening mind. The collection of wisdom is acquired by reflecting on the meaning of emptiness and by generating the wisdom understanding emptiness. Because understanding of suchness—phenomena's emptiness of intrinsic existence—is so important, we should all make an attempt to develop it. Of course, it is initially difficult to meditate on the meaning of emptiness, but if we make an attempt then we will gradually develop the ability to do so. (The meaning of emptiness is discussed in chapter 8.) Through this dual practice of collecting merit and wisdom we will gradually attain the fully awakened state of Buddhahood.

In order to protect our practice of the awakening mind from degenerating, we should observe four positive practices. The first is not intentionally telling lies. Of course, there may be occasions involving the safety and welfare of other people when we can sometimes tell a lie. That would be the practice of a bodhisattva.

Otherwise, we should not intentionally tell lies. We meet many people who deceive other people and tell lies as a matter of habit, which is very unfortunate.

The second positive practice is to be honest and avoid deceit. You should avoid hypocrisy. Do not lead other people to believe you have certain qualities you do not have. The third is to regard bodhisattvas as the actual Buddha. Praise their qualities and rejoice in them. Similarly, declare your admiration for the qualities of bodhisattvas, and, fourth, encourage other people to work toward the achievement of Buddhahood. Never discourage them by saying things like, "How do you expect to achieve Buddhahood, since you have neither the intelligence nor the perseverance?" If you observe these positive activities, you will never deceive your spiritual teacher or friends, nor will you allow other people to feel discouraged about their own practice of the Dharma.

If you manage not to tell lies, to be honest, to praise the Buddhas and bodhisattvas, and to inspire others to work toward the achievement of Buddhahood, then naturally the four corresponding negative activities will cease. I do not think this is too difficult if you try. In short, be a kind, warmhearted person, and for the rest of your life try to help other people. If you are unable to help them, at least refrain from harming them. If you lead an honest and meaningful life now, the future life will take care of itself.

CHAPTER 7

TRANSFORMING TROUBLE

INTO FORTUNE

*Transforming adverse circumstances into the
path to enlightenment is one of the most
powerful and unique instructions of the*

mind training teachings. Since our lives are beset by different kinds of difficulties and hardships, such teachings are extremely valuable. In this degenerate era, it is very hard to pursue the spiritual endeavor. Therefore, we need to develop certain techniques that can help us transform interfering forces into friends, harmful elements into spiritual teachers, and adverse circumstances into favorable ones. This kind of wisdom or skill is extremely beneficial.

Everything in life, good or bad, happiness or sorrow, success or failure, must be viewed in proper perspective. Nothing is purely black and white; all has different shades and degrees. If misfortune is viewed from a negative angle, it is naturally disheartening and painful. It is therefore essential to learn how to take a more positive view. You can compare your misfortune to those who are more miserable and acknowledge that you have been spared that greater misfortune. Such an attitude helps to reduce the burden and yields more insight into the nature of suffering. You also become more broad-minded and more relaxed. On the other hand, people who are unable to view their problems flexibly become depressed and unhappy. It is obvious that our minds have a great role to play in making our lives more meaningful and happier. This is not a question of achieving great spiritual feats but a matter of basic common sense.

The mind training teachings, as their name implies, chiefly concern ways and means of shaping the mind. This is particularly relevant to a Dharma practitioner. Unless we are able to train our minds so that they can withstand the ups and downs of life, it will be hard to continue our spiritual endeavor. Two situations can hamper our Dharma practice. One is when we are well off and everything goes smoothly with no obvious hindrances. The other is when we are beset by continual hardships and disasters. In the first case the mind becomes inflated and arrogant. This leads to other disturbing emotions, like jealousy and competitiveness. We must not allow ourselves to be carried away by the wind of such negative forces. On the contrary, we should learn to turn the situation to our advantage. It would be wiser to take a more wholesome view and reflect that we are able to enjoy good fortune and comfort now because of our past good actions. We can make a wish that others enjoy the same. When we are faced with various difficulties and misfortunes, we can easily become depressed. This is when we must be particularly careful and resilient. Otherwise our problems can overwhelm us and we may lose our hope and direction. It is important to recognize these two potentially disruptive situations and prepare accordingly.

One of the most distinctive and attractive characteristics of the Buddha's doctrine is the light it sheds on disturbing emotions. No other doctrine goes so deeply or into such fine detail in revealing the nature of delusion and disturbing emotions and how to deal with them. Numerous philosophical treatises portray disturbing emotions as our chief foe. Great emphasis is placed on our not giving in to disturbing emotions but fighting back. We are constantly advised how to evade the control of disturbing emotions. There is no occasion when disturbing emotions can be helpful to ourselves or others. On the contrary, disturbing emotions harm each and every one of us regardless of our social status, whether we are rich or poor. Disturbing emotions make no distinction between male or female, young or old, healthy or ailing. They are a source of confusion. Disturbing emotions cause individuals to lose their sense of humor, their judgment, and even their sanity. Under the sway of disturbing emotions, the most gentle-mannered person behaves outrageously. Cultured people become uncouth. Disturbing emotions are always negative and harmful. Buddhism teaches a wide variety of techniques to subdue and control the disturbing emotions. Its scriptures are concerned with waging war against disturbing emotions. The person who emerges victorious becomes a Buddha.

The practice of Dharma has two functions: increasing virtue and eliminating disturbing emotions. By and large, our whole being is so dominated by disturbing emotions that we hardly notice their presence. But when we begin to practice the Dharma and try to wage war on the disturbing emotions, we meet with interesting experiences. Initially the practitioner feels that negativities have increased and the mind has become more polluted with neurotic thoughts. If this happens to you, it is important to realize that in this case perception does not conform to reality. It is a sign that you are on the right track. Before entering into spiritual practice, you have no idea of the myriad games played by disturbing emotions. You only begin to be aware of them once you start to practice the Dharma. For instance, someone who suffers serious injury hardly feels the pain at the beginning, but under treatment that person will start to feeling agony as his or her senses recover.

Although the purpose of our spiritual endeavor is to gain freedom from problems and enjoy peace and success, things might not work out as intended. It may happen that we seem to experience greater hardship and increased difficulties. At such a juncture, you should not allow narrow considerations to dominate but should view things in a broader context. It may be that due to your Dharma practice, some aspect of your negative karma might have ripened earlier than it would otherwise have done. When this occurs, you can view it as a form of purification.

There are of five kinds of advice that support the practice of mind training. The first is to transform adverse situations into the path to enlightenment. The "Seven Point Mind Training" says,

> When the environment and its inhabitants
> overflow with unwholesomeness,
> Transform adverse circumstances into the path to
> enlightenment.

As many texts on logic explain, because every single phenomenon has countless aspects, much depends on what angle you view it from. For example, when you encounter suffering, if you think only of suffering, then it is intolerable. But if you forget that aspect, you may be able to see it from another angle. By enduring suffering you can purify your past negative actions and generate the determination to free yourself from the cycle of existence. Therefore, it is not true to say that suffering remains the same from any angle. The nature of suffering changes, depending upon your mental attitude and the way you look at it. If you are able to transform adverse situations into factors of the spiritual path, hindrances will become favorable conditions for spiritual practice. Through accustoming your mind to such a practice, you will meet with success and nothing will hinder your spiritual progress. It is said that being able to transmute adverse situations in this way is a sign that you are really undergoing spiritual training.

Taking adverse situations onto the path can be done in two ways: by relying on the incomparable thought of the awakening mind and by relying on the special practices for purifying negativities and accumulating virtue. Here the line from the text says,

Reflect immediately at every opportunity.

In good times or bad times, whether you are rich or poor, happy or unhappy, whether you are staying in your own or a foreign country, in a village, a city, a monastery, or an isolated place, whoever is accompanying you, whatever kinds of suffering you encounter, you should reflect that there are many other sentient beings encountering similar sufferings. And you can go on to think, "May the suffering I am undergoing serve to counter the sufferings experienced by other sentient beings. May they be parted from suffering."

As we discussed in relation to the practices of giving and taking, here you should think that the purpose of your meditating on compassion has been fulfilled, and rejoice. Also, when you are comfortably off and you have an abundance of food and clothing, a good house, good friends and teachers, and you are healthy, reflect that this is the result of past virtue. Then resolve to continue accumulating virtue in order to continue to enjoy such prosperity.

In our daily lives it is important to cheer ourselves up when we encounter suffering and become dispirited. Similarly, we need to come down to earth when we get too excited. If you have the courage to face adversity and problems, they will not disturb your mental balance. Some people lose their spirit when they become poor, others become conceited when they acquire a little wealth. In the face of happiness or suffering, it is best to remain stable.

With regard to taking adverse situations onto the path by relying on the special practices for purifying negativities and accumulating virtue, the line from the text says,

> The supreme method is accompanied by the four
> practices.

The first practice is accumulating merit. When you make offerings in order to create merit, the materials you use are not that important. What is significant is your attitude. You should develop an attitude of sharing whatever prosperity you have with others. Dedicate your merit to the common benefit of all sentient beings and direct your aspirations to the attainment of Buddhahood. The second practice is purifying negativities. Over beginningless time, impelled by disturbing emotions, we have accumulated misdeeds. As Milarepa said, the most important factor in purifying negativities is a strong sense of regret. The stronger your regret, the more forceful your purification will be. Similarly, it is important to resolve never to indulge in such actions again. The stronger your resolve, the more watchful you will be.

The third practice is making offerings to harmful spirits. You should intentionally think about the kindness of harmful spirits. A good practitioner would say, "Because you have been bothering me, I have been able to intensify my practice. The harm you have done has given me a great opportunity to test my patience, love, and compassion, so please don't relent." Instead of requesting them not to bother us, we urge them to continue to do so. It is said that if you respond with compassion and understanding, it not only protects you from harm but also decreases the force of the spirits' harmful intentions. There are many stories from the past in which spirits are said not to have harmed those who have strong compassion. The fourth practice is to seek the help of the Dharma protectors by making offerings to them. Arrange offerings of pure, clean materials. With a clear visualization, invite the Dharma protectors and guardians, make the offerings to them, and request them to assist you in incorporating adverse circumstances into the path.

The next section concerns how to accomplish the integrated practice of a single lifetime. The line from the mind training text says,

Train in the five powers.

First is the power of intention. Think, "From henceforth until I attain Buddhahood, at all times in this life until I die, particularly this year, this month, and this very day, I will be careful not to give any opportunity for disturbing emotions to arise induced by the misconception of self. I will not let my physical and verbal actions be dominated by them." Generally, whatever we are involved in, if planned systematically, it will be more successful. But success depends primarily on our firm intention.

Second is the power of the seed of virtuous practice. This means to preserve and enhance the precious awakening mind through giving, ethics, and meditation, making an effort to accumulate merit and wisdom.

Third is the power of countering negativity. This refers to the effort you make to uproot and eliminate negative forces like the self-centered attitude and the misconception of self that gives rise to it. Contemplating the harm such attitudes bring, you should develop a strong resolve never to let yourself fall under their sway.

Fourth is the power of prayer. Dedicate all that is good in the cycle of existence, especially the virtuous qualities you have gathered physically, verbally, and mentally in the three times (past, present, and future) to the welfare of all other sentient beings. At the end of every virtuous action, with awareness that it is empty of intrinsic existence, dedicate it to the welfare of sentient beings. At the end of every day, review your actions. If some negativities have been committed, develop strong regret and pray that through the power of virtue, you and all sentient beings may be able to generate the awakening mind and promote what one has already generated.

Fifth is the power of acquaintance. The great quality of the mind is that if you acquaint it with the practice and maintain the conditions for doing so, you will achieve perfection. As the saying goes, "There is nothing that does not become easier with acquaintance." The great spiritual teacher Che-ka-wa also said that this mind, which is full of faults, has one great quality—it complies with the way you train it.

You can also apply these five powers at the time of death. The text says,

> The five powers themselves are the Great Vehicle's
> Precept on the transference of consciousness.
> Cultivate these paths of practice.

At the time of death, these same five powers are applied in a different order and with a different intent. The first power is the power of the seed of virtuous practice. This refers to purifying faults and dedicating your possessions to the Buddha and suffering beings. Instead of remaining attached to your wealth, you should use it to accumulate virtue. All that is born is subject to death. Even a spiritual practitioner is not beyond the power of death. However, if you maintain a very powerful virtuous mind at the time of death, you can to some extent guarantee a better future life. Accustoming yourself to positive spiritual practices when you are alive and well makes it relatively easy to maintain a positive attitude at the time of death.

Nevertheless, it is possible to be quite familiar with virtuous practice but to be overcome by anger or attachment at the time of death. Then there is a great danger of taking a miserable rebirth. Therefore, we should try to transfer our consciousness to the next life peacefully, with calmness of mind. It is better not to cry, shout, and lament when someone is about to die, because that might stimulate anger or attachment within the dying person's mind.

When you have some control over your mind and energy flow, it is possible to stop the grosser processes of mind and energy and manifest the clear light, the most subtle level of consciousness. This will give rise to a better rebirth. If you are unable to do this, at least reflect on positive virtuous qualities as long as you remain conscious and do not dwell on negative thoughts. If you cannot even do that, it is important at least to have deep reverence and faith for your spiritual master and objects of refuge like the Buddha.

It is important to generate a virtuous state of mind at the time of death. Thus it is important to familiarize yourself with such a practice when you are alive and well. Without such preparation, if you are sick and overwhelmed with pain, it will be extremely difficult for you to focus on virtuous practices. Transference of consciousness is usually practiced when you have received a clear indication that you are going to die and there is no means of preventing it. Before your constituent elements disintegrate, you transfer your consciousness through spiritual practice. Since your experience in the next life will be determined to some extent by your motivation at the time of death, it is extremely important to have a positive motivation.

To undertake such a practice, purify all your faults through revealing and regretting your misdeeds. You will gain confidence that even if you die you have nothing to regret. Distribute your wealth and possessions to others so that at the time of death you will have no attachment toward them. Also cast off attachment to your body. This body to which you are attached is the basis for the misconception of self, because of which you have taken birth in the six realms of existence. And because of your attachment to food, clothing, and so forth, you have accumulated the ten unwholesome actions and the five perpetual misdeeds (killing one's mother, killing one's father, killing an arhat, intentionally wounding a Buddha, causing dissension in the Sangha). These are the cause for being thrown into the endless cycle of existence, where you encounter ceaseless suffering. Therefore, sever attachment to your friends, relatives, or your body.

The misconception of self is usually very strong at the time of death, because you fear losing your body. Therefore, try to establish the nature of the mind, its lack of intrinsic existence. This can mean two things: focusing on the clarity of the mind and focusing on its nature.

The second power at the time of death is the power of intention. You should approach death in a positive frame of mind. Continue to say your prayers and meditate on the stages of the dissolution of consciousness. Third is the power of countering negativity. Remembering the faults of delusions, determine never to let them overpower you. Fourth is the power of prayer.

Pray never to be separated from the awakening mind and not to be overcome by the misconception of self and the disturbing emotions that arise from it.

Fifth is the power of acquaintance. This concerns the physical procedure of lying on your right side, with your head toward the north, your right hand under your right cheek, with the ring finger stopping the breath from your right nostril. Place your left hand on your left thigh. This was the posture of the Buddha when he passed away. Because of the close link between mind and body, a relaxed physical posture helps to calm the mind at the time of death. Transfer your consciousness while meditating on the practice of giving and taking focused on your breathing. These practices vividly arouse love and compassion in your mind.

When it comes to gauging the extent to which we have trained the mind, the text says:

Integrate all the teachings into one thought.

The teachings contained in the various scriptures, whether they are the words of the Buddha or commentaries by his followers, have one purpose: to subdue the misconception of self. If you find that your activities, even your study and contemplation, serve as causes for increasing your misconception of self, this shows that your practice and study are going the wrong way. If you find, on the other hand, that your practice, study, and meditation are helping you overcome your misconception of self, this shows you are on the right track.

Primary importance should be given to the two
witnesses.

The real witness for your practice is not just other
people's judgment. You should constantly watch your
own mind, without deceiving yourself.

Constantly cultivate only a joyful mind.

If you are able to continue your practice of giving
and taking and remain happy, even when you meet
with hardship or you receive unpleasant news, your
practice of mind training has been successful.

The measure of a trained mind is that it has
turned back.

This implies a reversal of our normal reactions. For
example, our sense of permanence leads us to spend
our lives idly. We let our lives dwindle away. If, having
spent a day listlessly, you are filled with regret for the
wasted time, this reversal of the normal attitude is an
indication that your mind training is succeeding.
Whatever the circumstances, you will not waste your
precious human life but will extract meaning from it.
The same applies to the realization of emptiness. We
normally perceive things as existing intrinsically, but if
through our practice we have reversed this perception
and realized the lack of intrinsic existence, that is an
indication of having trained the mind.

There are five great marks of a trained mind.

The first of the five signs of greatness is seeing the awakening mind as the essence of all practice; this indicates that you have become a great bodhisattva. When you refrain from performing the slightest unwholesome deed because of your trust in the pattern of actions and results, you have become a great observer of discipline. When you are able to undergo any hardship in disciplining your mind and eliminating disturbing emotions, you have become a great ascetic. When you consistently behave in word and deed according to the conduct of the Great Vehicle, you have become a great practitioner of virtue. Finally, when your mind is constantly engaged in the yoga of generating the awakening mind and its auxiliary practices, you have become a great yogin.

> The trained mind retains control even when
> distracted.

Here, the spontaneous mental control of one who has trained the mind is likened to the skillful horseman who does not fall from his horse even when it bolts.

Concerning the commitments for those who are training their minds, the text says,

> Always train in the three general points.

This means that in training the mind, first, you should not contradict commitments related to your

other practices, such as your vows of individual liberation or bodhisattva vows. Sometimes people will say, "I
am engaged in the practice of mind training, so these
small things don't matter," when they break some
minor commitment. This directly contradicts the general practice of the Great Vehicle. A practitioner of
mind training should be able to integrate the essence of
all the Buddha's teachings into her or his own practice.

Second, simply because you are training your mind,
you cannot behave without due care. You cannot dig
into polluted earth, fell threatening trees, or disturb
noxious waters in the name of mind training. Nor can
you visit those people afflicted with contagious dis-
eases without precaution.

Third, when you are engaged in mind training, you
should be impartial. Whomever you deal with, whether
human or not, your relatives, friends, or enemies,
whether high or low, you should relate impartially toward all. Because you are training your mind for the
benefit of all sentient beings, you should generate love
and compassion toward all without discrimination.

Similarly, when it comes to countering the disturbing emotions, they are all to be eliminated. It is not
enough only to work on some of them. You should
know how antidotes are to be applied in general.

> Engage vigorously in forceful means to cultivate
> qualities and abandon disturbing emotions.

Generally speaking, we cannot use forceful methods to subdue beings, human or otherwise, because to

do so would only provoke their anger. But here we should use forceful methods against the disturbing emotions. Of these, the misconception of self is the most important, because it is the principal cause of suffering. Therefore, in the course of our spiritual practices of listening, thinking, and meditation, we should make every effort, whether physical, verbal, or mental, forcefully to transform the misconception of self.

We should be almost obsessive about removing the disturbing emotions. With deep resentment we should wage war against them. Since our disturbing emotions are so strong and deeply entrenched, the only way to destroy them is to turn the force of animosity, another disturbing emotion, against them. Even if it means being burned or killed or beheaded, you should never give in to the disturbing emotions.

Subjugate all the reasons (for selfishness).

To overcome our self-centered attitude, we first have to develop a strong sense of equanimity. Otherwise our natural tendency to discriminate between friends and enemies prevents us from cultivating an attitude of concern for the welfare of others.

Train consistently to deal with difficult
situations.

There are five relationships that are especially sensitive. In general, it is extremely serious to get angry or misbehave toward the Buddha, your abbot, those from whom you have received teaching, or your parents. It is important to avoid doing so. Second, you must be especially careful about generating disturbing emotions in relation to members of your own family, because these are the people you live with. Third, you need to be careful not to wish for misfortune to befall your rivals. Fourth, when people you are trying your best to help accuse you of neglecting them, you must restrain your anger. Should you become angry, you may not be able to generate compassion. Finally, there are sometimes people whom you instinctively dislike on sight although they have done nothing to harm you. Be careful not to become angry with them.

Don't rely on other conditions.

Whatever practices you do, such as listening, thinking, and meditating on the teaching, do not depend too much on external facilities.

Transform your attitude, but maintain your
    natural behavior.

Although it is good to meditate on the practice of the awakening mind and to bring about a mental transformation, you do not need to behave or speak strangely to show that you are a changed person. All our practices of mind training should be externally inconspicuous but internally should lead to great improvement. Now that we have entered the door of mind training, the text says,

Don't speak of others' faults,
Don't concern yourself with others' business.

You should neither find fault with others, human beings or otherwise, nor unkindly proclaim them in public.

Give up every hope of reward.

We engage in mind training with the intention of benefiting all other sentient beings, not wishing to lead a healthy life or enjoy better material facilities. Our primary aim is the attainment of Buddhahood for the benefit of all sentient beings.

Avoid poisonous food.

Although delicious food is meant to promote good health, when mixed with poison it can kill us. Similarly, by listening to, thinking about, and meditating on the Dharma, we are meant to attain the qualities of a Buddha. However, contaminating the practice and teaching of the instruction with worldly concerns and the misconception of self and a self-centered attitude is like murdering our chances of attaining liberation or the fully awakened state of a Buddha.

Don't maintain misplaced loyalty.

Maintaining inverted loyalty refers to allowing your good behavior to lapse when someone commits some slight wrong toward you. Holding a grudge and constantly hatching ill will toward them is improper. It blocks your chances of generating love and compassion.

Don't make malicious banter.

Do not argue with other people or use harmful words that strike at their hearts. It is improper, as the teacher Che-ka-wa said, to constantly remind people of the good you have done, especially when they were not aware of it in the first place.

Don't lie in ambush.

Do not nurse a grudge for some slight, waiting for an opportunity to retaliate. This kind of scheming attitude, waiting for the time to strike and relishing the chance to expose someone making a mistake, is completely contrary to the spirit of mind training.

Don't strike at the heart.

Digging up others' mistakes and revealing them is like striking at the vital point. This is the way to cause such suffering that the victim takes his or her own life. It is said that those who revel in disclosing others' faults have not a scent of the practitioner about them.

Don't put the load of a horse on a pony.

When you are unable to fulfill your responsibilities, you should not pass the burden to someone less able to bear it. Also, if you sense danger on the road, you should not take evasive action yourself while allowing your companion to continue in the same direction.

Don't sprint to win the race.

When you, as a member of a group, have rendered some favor, don't seek to take the gratitude for yourself.

Don't turn gods into devils.

If any aspect of your Dharma practice, in thought, word, or deed, serves to nourish your self-centered attitude, it is like turning gods into devils.

Don't seek others' misery as a means to happiness.

Neither use other people to achieve your own happiness nor rejoice at their misfortunes. There is every danger of us Tibetans doing this when we hear news of a disaster in China. Instead of feeling concern, we may feel a sense of satisfaction.

Concerning the precepts of mind training, the text says,

Every yoga should be performed as one.

Whether you are eating or getting dressed, whatever you do should be influenced by your practice of mind training.

There are two activities to be done at the
     beginning and end.

Whatever virtuous practices you do, at the beginning you should have the right motivation. At the end
of the day you should assess whether your actions have
been positive or negative. If they have been positive,
rejoice and congratulate yourself. If they have been
negative, repent and rebuke yourself. Another point is
that just as right motivation is important at the beginning, dedication is important at the end.

Train first in the easier practices.

If you think that taking on the sufferings of other
sentient beings and giving them your happiness and
virtuous qualities is difficult, do not give up. By training the mind gradually, you will become accustomed
to the practice.

Whichever occurs be patient with both.

Whether you encounter happiness or suffering of
body and mind, try to use them as a means to achieve
Buddhahood.

Guard both at the cost of your life.

Protect your commitments to your vows properly.
Be especially careful of the commitments of mind
training.

Train in the three difficulties.

First, it is difficult to remember the antidotes to the disturbing emotions. Second, disturbing emotions are difficult to stop. Third, it is difficult to cut their continuation. Therefore, identify the disturbing emotions, reflect on their faults from various angles, and make a constant effort to put a stop to them.

Transform everything into the Great Vehicle path.

When your activities are accompanied by love and compassion for sentient beings, motivated by a wish to attain Buddhahood, all your deeds of body, speech, and mind become a practice of the Great Vehicle.

Value an encompassing and far-reaching practice.

When training in the awakening mind, you should not be partial only toward a few sentient beings. Include all sentient beings of the four kinds of birth. Your practice should not be like a fisherman's visit to pray at a temple. A fisherman may go to the temple and pray for all beings but returns home and continues killing fish. His prayer carries little weight because his conduct contradicts the advice of the Buddha to whom he prays. His visit is little more than sightseeing. Your awakening mind should be pervasive, impartial, and extended toward all other sentient beings. Generally, we spontaneously utter sympathetic words when we see sentient beings suffering. Our practice should be not only on the verbal level but driven by heartfelt compassion.

When the great teacher Che-ka-wa was dying, he called his close disciple Se-chung-wa saying, "What a shame. Things won't work out as I hoped, so please make an offering to the Three Jewels."

Se-chung-wa asked, "What had you hoped for?"

Che-ka-wa replied, "Actually, I have always prayed that I would be able to gather the sufferings of all sentient beings at my heart like a pall of black smoke, but now I have only a vision of the Blissful Land, which is not what I wanted." This is how we should practice.

Similarly, when Gedun Gyatso, the Second Dalai Lama, was passing away, his disciples requested him to return to them saying, "Although you will be able to go to the Blissful Land, please sustain us by your kindness."

Gedun Gyatso replied, "As far as I am concerned, I have no aspiration to take rebirth in the Blissful Land but rather to take rebirth in an impure land where there are suffering sentient beings." This beautifully illustrates the bodhisattva's courage, taking responsibility for working for the welfare of others. Such practitioners aspire to be reborn wherever they could most effectively work for others.

Seek for the three principal conditions.

Whatever practice of hearing, contemplation, and meditation you do, the inner condition is life as a free and fortunate human being, equipped with the qualities of faith, wisdom, and effort. The external condition is to have found spiritual guidance. The circumstantial conditions include such facilities as adequate food and clothing. We should use these moderately. They should be neither too rich nor too poor. Our way of life should follow a middle path, free from either extreme.

It is important that ordained people especially do not lead too luxurious a life. But this is only one extreme; the other is to think that we can attain liberation by leading an overly ascetic life, neglecting our health, going about naked, and so forth. The ordained should wear their robes as prescribed, not clothes with decorations or long sleeves. Of course, if you are a tantric practitioner, you can keep your hair long. But all should observe their own prescribed disciplines. Monks are not supposed to have long hair. If their hair is long, we cannot be sure if a person is ordained or not.

We do all kinds of spiritual practice without much spiritual development. This is a clear indication that something is missing, something is lacking. If we have all the necessary external and internal conditions, as explained above, our spiritual qualities will develop like the waxing moon.

Purify the coarser ones first.

Try to eliminate the grosser levels of disturbing emotions first.

Practice that which is more effective.

Generally speaking, observing ethics is more important than extensive generosity. The practice of ethics is the basis for a stable mind. That peaceful, calm mind allows us to develop love and compassion. Love and compassion are healthy attitudes that leave us free from jealousy, fear, and anger. When we are subject to anger and fear, we readily pick quarrels with other people; then they too experience fear. This is because when we have hurt others, we naturally have to beware of them in case they try to retaliate.

The difference between anger and attachment is that anger leads to hurt and creates distance between you and others. Attachment draws them closer to you, but since it does not involve real concern for them, it also leads to problems in the end. All the disturbing emotions like attachment and anger prevent us from fully employing our unique human quality, our intelligence. It is said that many of our great debaters respond better when they are angry. But if the debater is calm, his or her answer is more likely to be clear.

Once we have seen the faults of the disturbing emotions, we should not allow them to reside within us. The special characteristic of Buddhist practice is always to seek the faults of the mind and remove them. When people who believe in an external creator run into trouble, they turn to the creator for help. This is not our custom. Instead, we should follow the unique practice of the Buddha and transform our minds.

"Practice that which is more effective" means that if we compare them, different aspects of practice are more important. We should not be satisfied with a certain level of realization but work to achieve the subsequent levels too. In the practice of mind training we start with the preparatory practices like reflecting on the rarity and potential of life as a free and fortunate human being. Having done that practice properly, you should add it to the factors inducing the awakening mind. Make an aspiration that this realization may serve as a factor for inducing the awakening mind within you. Think in the same way about your reflections on the faults of the cycle of existence. All the practices and meditations you undertake should contribute to enhancing your practice of the awakening mind.

Don't let three factors weaken.

Do not lose respect for your spiritual teacher. Do not let your mindfulness slacken. And do not lose the spirit of rejoicing in training the mind.

Never be parted from the three possessions.

Do not relinquish physical virtues such as paying proper respect to your spiritual master and the objects of refuge, by making prostrations, circumambulations, and so on. Do not give up verbal virtues, such as reciting prayers. Do not allow yourself to become parted from mental virtues, such as cultivating the awakening mind.

If you relapse, meditate on it as the antidote.

If your mind relapses or turns back to its old habits, you should use it as its own antidote. Having entered into the practice of mind training, people often say that they find more people are insulting them. Their misconception of self seems even stronger. Their disturbing emotions seem to be increasing. Facilities like food and clothing seem to be scarce. Some Tibetans may feel that although Tibet is a religious country, we have had to suffer the loss of our homeland, which might contribute to their losing faith in the Dharma. If you become weary and desperate like this, there is every possibility of relapsing into your old patterns of thought. At such times it is important to recognize how negative this is. Think instead, "Just as I have fallen prey to such despondency, many other sentient beings must find themselves in a similar crisis. How good it would be if the depression I have generated could take the place of all the disconsolate attitudes felt by other sentient beings."

Engage in the principal practices right now.

At this time practice is the most important thing you can do. Since you have found this precious human life, it is important to keep the next life in mind rather than work for this life alone. At this juncture you should undertake study and practice together. Of these two, the practice of meditation is the more important, because it is only by engaging in meditation that you can eventually overcome the obstructive factors in the mind. Without actual practice it will be difficult to receive the actual benefit. Sometimes when you are undergoing medical treatment you have to put up with great hardship. Parts of your body may even have to be amputated, but, faced with the need to survive, you do not dwell on these lesser sufferings. When you encounter certain hindrances in your training, it is a sign that you are penetrating the thick wall of disturbing emotions. Previously they were so overpowering that you were not aware of them. Because they are now being reduced through purification, you can see different categories of disturbing emotions.

Here it is very important to be discriminative. Just as Drom-tön-pa said, "Life is short but the range of knowledge is infinite. Therefore, just as swans extract milk from water when they are mixed together, choose what you think is best and most suitable for you to practice." If you go on explaining or studying the meaning without doing the practice, it will not be very helpful. Therefore, generate the awakening mind and its auxiliary practices now and pray not to be separated from it in future lives.

In the future always put on armor.

Guard your body, speech, and mind against engaging in negative deeds, and guard yourself against deterioration of your practice of awakening mind.

Do not apply a wrong understanding.

We should generate real compassion when sentient beings are afflicted by different levels of suffering. However, if we generate sympathy instead for those who are undergoing hardship while listening to, thinking about, or meditating on the Dharma, if we feel sorry for them, that is misplaced compassion because they are experiencing worthwhile hardship in the course of ultimately overcoming suffering. Our aspiration should be to attain Buddhahood, but if we aspire to mundane achievements such as public respect, that is wrong aspiration. We should be aiming to deliver all sentient beings to the state of Buddhahood, but if instead we simply take care of the offerings made to the objects of refuge and the spiritual community, that is wrong endeavor. We should rejoice in the virtues of the Buddhas and bodhisattvas from the depths of our hearts, and our own virtuous qualities will multiply. But to rejoice at the mishaps that befall someone we dislike is inappropriate rejoicing.

We should keep our patience for the hardships we encounter in the practice of the Dharma. If instead we indulge in worldly concerns, trying to help our friends and defeat our enemies, and then put up with the resulting sufferings, that is misplaced patience. Having entered the door of the Great Vehicle, we should taste the flavor of the doctrine by listening to it and thinking about it. If instead we develop a taste for sensual objects and the fruit of helping friends and relatives and harming enemies, that is wrong taste.

Don't be sporadic.

The practice of mind training should not be intermittent but constant.

Practice unflinchingly.

We have to practice straightforwardly, without hesitation.

Be liberated by examination and analysis.

Always be watchful and apply mental alertness.

Don't be boastful.

You might be helping other sentient beings in some small way, but to boast about it is contrary to the mind training precepts.

Don't be short-tempered.

If you find you lose your temper at the slightest provocation, restrain yourself and do not retaliate.

Don't make a short-lived attempt.

At the beginning you may be very enthusiastic, but if your enthusiasm wanes and becomes fleeting, it contradicts the mind training precepts. Your effort should be like the flow of a stream—sustained, continuous, and balanced.

Don't expect gratitude.

This refers to our wish for immediate reward. The great bodhisattva Che-ka-wa, having undertaken the practice of mind training in such a way that he achieved realization, said, "Even if I die, I have no regrets."

CHAPTER 8

THE AWAKENING VIEW

OF REALITY

The aim of the awakening mind is twofold—to attain enlightenment and to benefit all sentient beings. At the present

time many people would question whether Buddhahood is something individuals can achieve. This can be effectively answered when we understand that disturbing emotions are only temporary afflictions of the mind. There are powerful and effective opponents, such as the wisdom understanding emptiness, which can totally eradicate them. For this reason it is essential to understand the meaning of emptiness. This requires training, because emptiness does not imply a state of vacuity or nothingness. What are things empty of? According to the Middle Way school, all phenomena are empty of intrinsic existence.

Here, the process of first coming to understand emptiness and then familiarizing our minds with it is referred to as the ultimate awakening mind. It is called ultimate because it deals with the ultimate nature of phenomena. The text says that such instructions should be given to a suitable recipient, otherwise they could be harmful. The question is, how do you discriminate who is and who is not a suitable recipient? From seeing smoke we know there is fire, and from observing the way certain waterbirds behave in the air we know there is a lake nearby. So, by observing certain signs and characteristics we can understand a person's nature.

When we meet a spiritual master for the first time or hear certain instructions, sometimes we feel an unaccountable sense of bliss and contentment. That is an indication that we have some link with them from the past. One of the signs that a person is a suitable recipient for instruction about emptiness is that he or she feels a strong sense of faith on merely hearing the names of its great Indian proponents, Nagarjuna, Aryadeva, and Chandrakirti. Another is that on hearing an explanation of emptiness he or she develops a great interest and aspiration to know more about it.

The reason it is important to identify the right recipient for these instructions is that otherwise the instructions might lead people to the dangerous position of nihilism. When emptiness, or things' lack of intrinsic existence, is explained to certain people, they misunderstand it as saying nothing exists. There is then a danger that such people will mistakenly condemn the Buddha's doctrine.

Another kind of risk concerns people who have an interest in and admiration for the philosophy of emptiness because it has been praised by the great masters of the past. However, because they do not have a clear understanding of emptiness, they do not realize that it is in fact because things are empty of intrinsic existence that it is possible for them to function on the conventional level. If your understanding tends to identify emptiness with nothingness, there is a danger of thinking that the Buddhas, bodhisattvas, and everything else are simply empty, that they do not exist and thus are incapable of helping others. Then your relationship with the Buddha and the Three Jewels may not be effective.

If you explain the meaning of emptiness to those who are not ready, they may misunderstand and become afraid of the practice of emptiness. People who have heard a little about the meaning of emptiness may try to explain it to others by saying that since everything is naturally empty, nothing is good or bad. This is a great misinterpretation. Emptiness is not equivalent to total nonexistence. It refers to things being empty of intrinsic existence, which actually means that things arise in dependence on causes and conditions. Therefore, it is wrong to say that you can engage casually in any kind of activity because things are empty.

Drom-tön-pa once told someone that his hand was naturally empty and fire was also naturally empty. But that did not mean that if he put his hand in the fire it would not burn. This shows that both hand and fire do exist, since when we put our hand in the fire it burns. But the nature of that existence is dependent on many factors. When you understand emptiness in terms of dependent existence, it will be powerful and will inspire you to observe the law of cause and effect more strictly.

When instructions on emptiness are given to suitable recipients, their understanding of emptiness will complement their understanding of the way things arise in dependence on causes and conditions. Consequently, they will realize that in order to pursue their understanding of emptiness in future lifetimes, they will need to accumulate the necessary causes and conditions for taking favorable rebirth. Therefore, they will observe pure morality and engage in generosity, patience, and so forth. In this way their understanding of emptiness will augment their progress on the path to enlightenment.

Regarding the appropriate time to explain how to train in the ultimate awakening mind, the "Seven Point Mind Training" says,

> When stability has been attained, impart the secret teaching.

There are two kinds of practitioners. Some train in understanding emptiness first and then develop the conventional awakening mind. The others develop compassion and the conventional awakening mind first, which eventually leads to the realization of emptiness. The tradition being explained here follows the second process. First you think about the value of life as a free and fortunate human being and about death and impermanence. These create the perspective provoking you to engage in the actual practice of generating the awakening mind. Once you have gained stability in the practice of that path, the meaning of emptiness or ultimate truth is explained.

It is important first to acquire a good understanding of the different aspects of conventional existence, how things nominally exist. Then we examine how all these things that conventionally exist do not have intrinsic existence but exist only by designation, which means this: we can think about things having two aspects. One aspect is emptiness or lack of intrinsic existence, and the other is their being dependent on other factors. When we talk about something existing by designation, we are saying it does exist, against the notion of its total nonexistence, but that it exists only as designated by names and thought. The lines from the mind training text say,

> Consider all phenomena as like dreams,
> Examine the nature of unborn awareness.
> The remedy itself is released in its own place,
> Place the essence of the path on the nature of
>   the basis of all.

All phenomena are like a dream, because they are illusory in that they do not have true existence. Analyzing the ultimate nature of awareness, which is unborn, means learning that the wisdom understanding emptiness also does not have intrinsic existence. When you analyze its nature, the subjective mind also does not have intrinsic existence.

If you think about it in this way, the first line explains the lack of intrinsic existence of objects, or external phenomena. The second line explains the lack of intrinsic existence of the subject, consciousness, or internal phenomena. The continuity of the mind comes from beginningless time and is not produced by adventitious causes and conditions. Therefore it is called unborn. However, because it is a continuity of moments, that mind is also free from intrinsic existence. The third line explains that the observer or the person who analyzes is also empty of intrinsic existence. This is sometimes referred to as the emptiness of emptiness. Realization of emptiness is the antidote to the misconception of self. That emptiness is also, as it were, liberated in its own turn, because if you examine it, it does not have intrinsic existence either. Because there is a great danger of emptiness being regarded as permanent, absolute, and truly existent, the Buddha emphasized that it too should be understood as being without intrinsic existence.

These first three lines explain how to do analytical meditation. The last line explains that when you analyze in that way, you will not be able to find the independent or intrinsic existence of anything. And when you are unable to find it, you should meditate onepointedly, unhindered by laxity and excitement, on that very absence of intrinsic existence. Having reached an understanding of that absence through analysis, you let the mind dwell undistractedly on what you have understood in order to fully absorb it. When you analyze and are unable to find intrinsic existence, it does not mean that things do not exist at all, but that they do not have any independent existence. Things exist by depending on other things.

You can either rely on someone or not. The two ideas are mutually exclusive and opposed to each other. Previously, due to misconception, you thought that things existed independently. But when you examine the issue and look for independent or intrinsic existence, you are unable to find it. Things do exist, because we experience happiness and suffering in relation to them. Since under analysis you are unable to find their intrinsic existence, their existence is clearly dependent on other factors. Thus things do not have independent existence.

When you are able to negate independent existence through this process, you will gain a clear apprehension of the mere absence of intrinsic existence. At that point, without engaging in any further analysis, simply meditate single-pointedly on what you have understood. Of course, this does not necessarily mean that you never engage in any analysis again. I think the emphasis here is to use single-pointed concentration more than analysis.

Next, the text explains how to continue the practice after the meditation session:

In between meditation sessions, be like a conjuror, a creator of illusions.

This completes the short explanation of the meaning of the lines in the "Seven Point Mind Training." However, the author of our text goes on to give a more elaborate explanation. For this he turns to the tradition of the great Indian spiritual teachers such as Nagarjuna, Aryadeva, and Chandrakirti. This was also the Tibetan master Tsong-kha-pa's approach.

First we need to identify ignorance, which is the root of the cycle of existence. After that we will establish the meaning of selflessness. We come across the word *ignorance* many times in these kinds of instructions. Usually *ignorance* means a lack of knowledge, so there are various categories of ignorance. In the context of the process known as the twelve links of dependent arising, ignorance comes first. This means that if you have ignorance, the remaining links in the process of dependent arising will occur. As a result, you will take rebirth in the cycle of birth and death.

What is this ignorance? It is the opposing factor that contradicts awareness or knowledge. It is not just something other than awareness, nor is it the mere absence of awareness. It is the complete opposite of awareness or knowledge, with awareness referring specifically to the wisdom understanding that there is no self, no independent existence.

Ignorance involves two kinds of misconception of self: that of persons and that of phenomena. We discriminate between persons and phenomena because the person is the one who enjoys or observes. All the possessions and other objects related to the person are phenomena. It is the person who wants to achieve liberation and enjoy happiness. Due to ignorance or the misconception of self within us, we first seize on our own selves as intrinsically existent. We then identify our belongings as "mine." The object of the misconception of self in relation to persons is the conventional "I." And the objects of the misconception of self in relation to phenomena are conventional phenomena. Ignorance exaggerates these objects, seeing persons and phenomena as existing independently or intrinsically.

In order to establish selflessness, we need to negate these exaggerations. But we must be careful to identify just what we are seeking to negate. If we fail to differentiate between true existence and conventional existence, we will go too far and negate existence in general. We will be unable to assert even the valid existence of persons and phenomena. As a result we will be unable to demonstrate the existence of the path and the resultant fully awakened state of the Buddha. We will also be unable to justify the infallibility of the principle of cause and effect.

Similarly, we should not underestimate what is to be negated. That is to say, we should not negate too little. All Buddhist philosophical schools accept what are known as the four seals. The Buddha taught, first, that all composite phenomena are transitory, which means that everything is dependent on other factors. Second, all contaminated things are miserable. This does not mean that we have simply to give in to suffering, because the third seal is that all phenomena are selfless. They are empty of intrinsic existence; they do not have true existence. Although this is their true nature, because of our misconceptions, we see phenomena as existing independently. If you understand this, you will be able to find the path to liberation, or the way out of the cycle of existence. The fourth seal states that nirvana or liberation is peace. These four points actually summarize the Buddha's instructions.

Depending on how selflessness is explained, there are also differences in the way the disturbing emotions are accounted for. All but the school of Chandrakirti say that ignorance is the root of the cycle of existence. But they define it as intellectually acquired ignorance, which means it is the result of mistaken philosophical ideas. However, these kinds of misconception only influence people who have studied philosophy. If that were the case, how could we account for the presence in the cycle of existence of beings whose minds are not influenced by the study of philosophy?

The great Indian teacher Chandrakirti challenged this point. He refuted the notion that the ignorance at the root of the cycle of existence is only based on philosophy, because such ignorance is found even within animals who have no opportunity to study. He said animals can be seen to be involved with the misconception of an "I." If the object to be negated is confined to intellectually acquired ignorance, it will be too narrow and liberation will not occur. According to Chandrakirti, the ignorance at the root of the cycle of existence is innate.

According to the Middle Way school of Chandrakirti, even though things have relative or conventional existence, it is not necessary that they should be found to exist under fine analysis. According to this interpretation, when you subject a phenomenon to such analysis you cannot find it existing of its own accord. Because you are unable to find it standing autonomously, the conclusion is that things arise in dependence on other causes and conditions.

Therefore, phenomena are said to validly exist as designated by names and thought. This does not mean that your mind can fabricate anything it likes, that you can create anything like a magician. The meaning of the emptiness of intrinsic existence is existence in dependence on other factors, and the meaning of dependent arising is emptiness. Therefore, Nagarjuna has said that knowing the empty nature of all phenomena and relying on the principle of actions and their results is the most wonderful practice.

According to this explanation, the way the misconception of self apprehends its object is as follows. Whether the object is a person or a physical entity, if you see that object not as merely designated by the mind but as having an objective existence, that is the object to be negated. The absence of such existence in relation to the person is called the selflessness of the person, and the absence of such existence in relation to the body and other physical entities is called the selflessness of phenomena. The self is something that has intrinsic existence without depending on others. The absence of this is selflessness. And selflessness is of two kinds: selflessness of persons and selflessness of phenomena.

To understand the concept of phenomena as designated—dependent on mere names and concepts—we might look at the example of the rope and the snake. Seeing a coiled rope at dusk, you might mistake it for a snake. As a result you feel very afraid. Although there is no snake there at all, because of the shape and color of the coiled rope at nightfall and due to your own misconceptions, you think it is a snake and feel fear. Approaching the coil of rope, you will find it possesses not the slightest quality of a snake in terms of color, shape, and so forth; you are unable to find a snake in the coil of rope. Similarly, even though we call ourselves such and such, if we try to analyze who we really are and try to find that person within our collection of physical and mental components, we will be unable to find it. Just as the snake does not exist in that coiled rope, phenomena do not exist in their own right, "out there" in the objects themselves.

We are mistaken in our designation when we misperceive the coiled rope as a snake; we will not be able to find any snake when we search on the basis of that label. Similarly, we may talk of a person and his or her belongings, but when we search for the real person, we do not find it. Still, whether we give that person a Tibetan name, an Indian name, or an English name, something is being referred to. But when we search for it analytically, not being satisfied with the label and concept alone, we will not find it.

This shows that nothing exists in its own right. But it is not an indication that things do not exist at all, because we can relate to them. Since they exist only on the conventional or relative level, we can only say they exist by means of designation. After misapprehending a snake on the basis of the coiled rope, we search but do not find any aspect of snake in the coiled rope—not in the collection of its parts, not in the actual rope itself, and not even in a part of the rope.

The snake imputed to the coiled rope does not exist. However, the self posited on the basis of the person's collection of physical and mental components does exist. Therefore, things do not exist merely because they are mentally created. So, the question is, why is it that when we posit the label *snake* on the basis of the body of the snake, the snake exists, but when we apply the label to a coiled rope, it does not exist? What is it that distinguishes the two? The difference is that when the label is posited on the basis of the body of the snake, it complies with convention, so it exists on a conventional level. When the label *snake* is applied on the basis of a coiled rope, it is not accepted even conventionally. Thus when we talk about the "I" or self, whatever phenomenon we choose to examine, there is no substantial entity from the side of the object. Phenomena are dependent on other causes and conditions; therefore they do not exist of their own accord.

They have no intrinsic existence. In other words, there is no self-existence.

Whether it is the Buddha, a sentient being, or a house, whatever it is, when we search for it among its parts we do not find it. This shows that things exist only in dependence on names and concepts. When you have thought about that and come to some understanding of it, relate it to your own experience. Watch how things appear to you. They tend not to appear as though they were designated by our names and concepts, but as though they had an intrinsic, independent status in their own right. This shows that there is a discrepancy between the way things appear to us and the way things exist in reality. First think about this in terms of identifying the object to be negated, which is the object's existing in its own right. Then think about the way in which things actually do exist, in dependence on mere names and concepts.

Right from form up to the nature of the Buddha, things exist by depending on other causes and conditions. Therefore, every phenomenon lacks intrinsic existence. Even emptiness has no independent existence, so we talk about the emptiness of emptiness. All phenomena are devoid of intrinsic existence. Accordingly, having intrinsic existence, having existence by its own nature or in its own right, having ultimate existence, having true existence, and having real existence all mean the same. They are all objects to be negated.

When you meditate on the meaning of selflessness, you should examine how the innate misconception of self arises within your mind. It is the innate misconception that is important here rather than misconceptions induced by studying mistaken philosophy. To have a good understanding, you need to rely on a spiritual teacher. Now to examine your innate sense of self, you have to be watchful. Sometimes when someone rebukes you or insults you or accuses you, it upsets you. You feel, "How dare he say that!" At that time your innate self will pop up. Similarly, this innate self will appear when you have strong feelings of attachment or anger. This does not mean that the innate sense of self arises only on those occasions, of course; it is usually with us. But on such occasions it is easier to catch hold of.

The point here is to pay attention to how this sense of innate self appears in our own experience. Times of strong attachment, pride, or indignation are particularly apt. Another approach is to study a text that explains the nature of the self and selflessness and that will give you grounds for analysis. When you examine the nature of the self in that way, you will come to the conclusion that it cannot be found. Your not being able to find it does not indicate its total nonexistence, because you know from your own experience that it exists conventionally. When you have gained some understanding of how things exist as designated by name and thought, you should again observe how things normally appear to you. By comparing your understanding with your experience you will be able to get a clearer picture of the nature of phenomena—that things arise in dependence on causes and conditions and not independently.

Normally, everything appears to us through our sense consciousnesses or our mental consciousness. And everything appears to have its own independent existence. However, through study and observing our own experience, we can gradually come to understand the meaning of selflessness. Thereafter, study and experience of how things appear will reinforce the understanding that things do not arise independently. It is important on the one hand to study what is explained in books, but you must also assess how things appear to you in normal daily life.

Now, how does this ignorance serve as the root of the cycle of existence? The innate notion of an intrinsically existent self gives rise to the notion of belongings, identifying them as "mine." This in turn gives rise to attachment, thus inducing us to engage in negative actions, which in turn produce rebirth in the cycle of existence. Rebirth is dependent upon karmic actions, which themselves are induced by disturbing emotions. For example, desire for "my happiness" prevents us from seeing the faults of such an attitude. Therefore, it is our innate tendency to think of "I" and "mine" as intrinsically existent that serves as the root of the cycle of existence.

In order to eliminate the misconception of self, you must establish the view of selflessness. The way to do this is to understand the way ignorance apprehends its object and to come to the conclusion that the object of such misapprehension is nonexistent. In making your mind familiar with that understanding, you will be able to remove the misconception of self. Unless you realize the nonexistence of the object of ignorance, you will not be able to remove the misconception of self itself. The seed or root of the cycle of birth and death is the ignorance that conceives of true existence. It is only by dispelling that through the realization of emptiness that we will be able to prevent rebirth into the cycle of existence. When we are tired from overwork we rest. Although that helps temporarily, it does not actually resolve the real problem. Overcoming the problem requires facing up to it and actually resolving it. Similarly, ignorance cannot be eliminated simply by shutting your mind off, as some proponents of nonconceptual meditation suggest. Rather, you must meditate on the wisdom understanding emptiness. If you meditate on something else, your meditation will be irrelevant.

It is only through constant familiarity with the analysis negating intrinsic existence that you will be able to realize emptiness and undermine ignorance. Simply thinking that things are empty by nature and do not have inherent existence will not help eliminate ignorance. If you identify every type of conceptual experience as ignorance, it implies that any conscious experience amounts to ignorance misconceiving the true nature of phenomena. This is not the case, because the conceptual thought that conceives a person as a person is valid, whereas the conceptual thought that conceives someone seen in a dream as a person is mistaken. Although both these consciousnesses have in common the lack of true existence, it is important to discriminate between the two. One is a valid experience, and the other is invalid. Similarly, the Buddha, sentient beings, the cycle of existence, and the state beyond sorrow are the same in the sense that they lack intrinsic existence. Still, you must be able to discriminate between those that are objects to be aspired to and those that are to be discarded or avoided.

How is the view of selflessness to be established? The self of persons and the self of phenomena are both objects to be negated. There is no difference between them in terms of subtlety. But because of some difference of subtlety in the nature of the object, it is said that the selflessness of persons is more easily realized.

In order to establish the selflessness of persons, you must first understand what is meant by self or person. There are different interpretations of this according to the various Buddhist schools of thought. The actual object of the conception of self is "I." This is something that exists conventionally, as a designated phenomenon, labeled on the basis of the physical and mental components. According to Chandrakirti, none of the collection of physical and mental components could be the person. He says we generate a feeling of "I" in relation to our physical and mental components, but we do not see any of them as "I." We think of them as "mine." For example, we look at our legs and say, "Those are my legs." We do not identify ourselves completely with our legs or our minds or any other of our physical and mental components.

From these examples we move to the understanding that the person is the mere label designated upon the basis of the physical and mental components. The physical makeup of the person is composed of all these different elements, which individually are not the person. Nor is the collection of these physical and mental components the person. Still, there is no person unrelated to and separate from these components. Therefore, the person exists merely as a label or designation. Identifying how the self or person exists as a label or designation reveals that it lacks independent or intrinsic existence. This is what is meant by establishing the selflessness of persons. So, it is said that the deeper your understanding of the way in which things are posited merely as labels and designations, the deeper is your understanding of emptiness.

There are two ways to present the selflessness of the person. Showing that there is no intrinsically existent "I," and showing that nothing exists intrinsically as "mine." The ultimate nature of the self is a phenomenon that we cannot experience directly. Generally speaking, phenomena are of different types. Some are very obvious and can be perceived directly. They require no logical proof. Other types of phenomena are beyond our direct experience. To perceive them we need to depend on some kind of logical reasoning. Emptiness falls into this category; it is something that needs to be approached through logical reasoning. If your understanding of selflessness is confined only to believing what the Buddha said—his mere words—it will not be correct.

To establish the "I" as having no intrinsic existence, you first examine your own mind and identify the way the innate conception of self apprehends its object. There are two methods for doing this: analytical meditation and single-pointed meditation. Analytical meditation, which we are engaged in here, is done using different patterns of logic. If the "I" exists as we identify it, as intrinsically existent, it must be either one with our physical and mental components or separate from them. There are only these two possibilities with no option in between. If the "I" had an independent existence, it could not depend on the person's physical and mental components. Either the physical and mental components are the "I" themselves, or the "I" has no relation to them at all. If the physical and mental components are the "I," when they disintegrate at death, the "I" will also disintegrate. Similarly, just as a person leaves her body behind when she dies, the "I" will also be abandoned. Furthermore, if the "I" were truly one with the physical and mental components, as there are many components, there would be many selves within one person.

If the self or "I" of this life and the next life have no relation between them, they would not be of the same continuum. The virtuous actions done by the person of this life would not affect the continuity of his next life. In that case, whatever the person in the next life experiences would be without cause or condition because he would not have created the experiences himself, since he is not related to the person of the previous life. In this way you can see the faults of holding the view that the person is either truly one with or separate from his or her physical and mental components. That realization leads to the understanding that there is no intrinsically existent, truly existent, or independent person. When you have ascertained that, you have realized the selflessness of the person.

Next, you can establish the lack of intrinsic existence of "mine." Refuting the existence of an intrinsic or independent self leads to understanding the lack of independent existence of its belongings too. There is no need to go through different processes of reasoning. For as Nagarjuna put it, "If the self does not (intrinsically) exist, how will 'mine' exist?" Similarly, having established the lack of an intrinsically existent "I" in relation to yourself, you can extend the logic to understand the selflessness of other persons too.

In establishing the selflessness of phenomena, identifying the object to be negated is similar to what was explained concerning the selflessness of persons. Here again you apply the reasoning of the absence of singularity and plurality. You simply change the focus from the person to a phenomenon such as your body or a book and determine that it also is not ultimately one or many. Phenomena such as the physical and mental components of a person are free from being truly one or many because they have parts. Therefore, they do not have innate existence. Within our physical body we have internal elements, and, similarly, we also depend on external elements. The dependent relationship between them is easy to understand. All phenomena have parts and there is no phenomenon that is partless. If something has form it has parts, because it extends in various directions. If it is formless like consciousness, its parts are the various moments of its continuity.

Understanding this makes the reasoning of dependent arising easier to understand. Although phenomena have conventional, nominal existence, if you search for a phenomenon analytically, you will be unable to find it. By this means, too, we can come to understand dependent arising, which means that things exist as designated. When you realize the meaning of dependent arising, you will also understand that things do not have independent existence. If things exist independently, they cannot arise in dependence on others. No phenomenon arises in dependence on others and also has independent existence.

A good example of dependent arising is when you see the reflection of your face in a mirror. Many causes and conditions come together to make it possible to see your reflection, such as the presence of the mirror. When you look into the mirror you see a reflection of your face, yet you know that the image of your face is not your true face. Similarly, things arise in dependence on causes and conditions, yet they do not have independent existence. Of all the various kinds of reasoning used to establish emptiness, the most important is the reasoning of dependent arising. As we have already discussed, if we hold harmful intentions toward others, it will only harm us. And if we hold beneficial attitudes toward others it will help both others and ourselves. This shows that there is a relationship between attitudes and their consequences. Similarly, due to our long habituation with the misconception of self and different kinds of disturbing emotions in the past, their effects are felt within this lifetime. These are ways in which dependent arising can be understood through our own experience.

Since all phenomena exist only in dependence on other factors, they cannot be independent. External phenomena are dependent upon their parts. Consciousness can be posited only on the basis of collection of moments in a continuum. Certain phenomena can only be posited in dependence on each other, like action and agent. Parent and child are mutually dependent in the same way. Someone is only a parent because he or she has children, and a daughter or son is so called only in relation to parents. When we analyze this we will see, for instance, that a man becomes a father only when he has a child. But we tend to presume that the father comes first. Even in terms of the names of trades the same applies. A tailor is so called because of the action of tailoring.

If we try to go deeper into this and search for the essence of the name, we do not find anything. Contradictions and frustrations arise, because although things exist only as mere labels and imputations, we relate to them as if they were independent and existed in their own right. Being dependent or independent is a mutually exclusive dichotomy. There is no third possibility. Since everything is dependent by nature, it cannot be independent. As the self purports to be independent, the very absence or negation of that independent status is selflessness or emptiness. If we take our understanding of dependent arising to its subtlest and deepest level, we will reach an understanding of emptiness. If you do not have an empty space you cannot construct a building. Similarly, if phenomena were not empty by nature, they could not possess so many different qualities. So, understanding of emptiness of intrinsic existence can inspire understanding of dependent arising. And when you reflect on dependent arising, it will lead immediately and automatically to an understanding of emptiness.

It is right and proper to explain dependent arising and the emptiness of intrinsic existence using a single object, so that understanding of the emptiness of that object reinforces understanding of its dependent arising. On the other hand, if your understanding of emptiness decreases your understanding of dependent arising, there is something wrong with your approach. When your understanding of the two is complementary and mutually reinforcing, you will be able to understand both on the basis of one object alone. It is said that it is common to all the philosophical schools that appearances dispel the extreme of nihilism and emptiness dispels the extreme of absolutism.

When we are involved in meditation on emptiness there are two disruptive factors to avoid: the extreme views of absolutism and nihilism. The distinctive feature of the reasoning of dependent arising is that it has the power to dispel both these extremes simultaneously. The text says that emptiness of intrinsic existence pervades everything from form up to the fully awakened mind. It is not a mere philosophical postulation, nor is it a nihilistic view, because understanding of it will lead to the understanding of dependent arising. It is an object of the wisdom that realizes the ultimate nature of phenomena. Realization of it leads to eliminating the two obstructions—disturbing emotions and the obstructions to omniscience.

How do you undertake this practice during the stabilizing meditation? Some advocate meditating only on a nonconceptual state of the mind. Others teach simply withdrawing the mind from the object of negation. But neither of these approaches is enough. But if you employ analysis and are unable to find the existence of the self in its own right, that is the point on which you must sustain your meditation. To meditate on the selflessness of persons, you should know how the misconception of self conceives of the "I" as having intrinsic existence, or existence from its own side. It is not enough simply to say that the "I" does not exist in this or that way. It is important that you first have a clear awareness of the object to be negated. Then you should refute the existence of the object to be negated, that is the self, without which you will not be able to realize selflessness.

All the miseries we undergo are caused by ignorance, the object of which is an intrinsically existent self. Emptiness of intrinsic existence is the mere negation or absence of that self. Therefore, in meditation, first identify the object to be negated, the intrinsically existent self. Establish selflessness on the basis of that.

Hold that realization of selflessness as your object of meditation, and let your mind be absorbed by it without affirming anything. This absorptive single-pointed meditation should be maintained with a strong awareness of the selflessness of the person. This should be reinforced by repeated application of analysis. Reflect again and again on the reasonings to prove selflessness. You must always retain the force of the ascertainment. If the force of what you have ascertained slackens, but you remain in absorption, it will not be meditation on emptiness. If the practitioner first properly identifies the object to be negated, then refutes it through reasoning and apprehends that negation, cultivating a strong ascertainment, that will be a proper understanding of emptiness. Otherwise, simply to keep on thinking that things do not exist intrinsically, without having properly identified the object to be negated, will not yield a proper understanding.

How do you cultivate mental tranquillity, a calmly abiding, one-pointed mind? One way is by training in ethics, which in this case refers to guarding the practitioner from the influence of the self-centered attitude. Another is the training in wisdom, understanding the emptiness of intrinsic existence. But experiencing that kind of wisdom only once or twice is not sufficient. It is important to develop clarity on the basis of that realization. You have to cultivate it until it is spontaneous. This can be done only by developing constant familiarity through meditation, leading eventually to a direct perception of emptiness. To do this, you must practice single-pointed concentration. Otherwise your understanding of emptiness will not be stable or firm. Having applied this calmly abiding mind to the meaning of selflessness, engage in analysis of selflessness again. Then gain familiarity with the technique for balancing a calmly abiding mind with discriminating awareness. When you derive a fresh pliancy or flexibility from the impact of analytical meditation, you will have achieved special insight. Now, the text says,

> In between meditation sessions, be like a conjuror,
> a creator of illusions.

How are we to understand this? It is said that when you arise from single-pointed meditation, solid phenomena like rocks and hills may appear in a slightly different way, as if they were creations of your own mind. That is not what is meant by illusion here.

The real way everything appears as illusory is when you see it as like a mirage, an illusion or dream, so that you do not see anything as having intrinsic or independent existence. From forms up to the fully awakened mind, you should see all phenomena as being like illusions. During the actual meditation session, you negate the intrinsic existence of phenomena and see emptiness as in the nature of space. When you arise from meditation, you view phenomena as illusory or deceptive. Although they lack true existence, still they project an appearance of being truly existent. So there is a contradiction between the way things exist and the way they appear to us. Maintaining an awareness of this is the real meaning of seeing things as like illusions here. It is said that after you have realized emptiness, it is not necessary to make a special effort for things to appear as like illusions; it occurs naturally.

The author says that in the past certain scholars mistook the meaning of the example of an illusion. They interpreted it to imply that things do not exist at all. They said that although persons appear as persons, in reality they are not persons, and so forth. This is mistaken understanding of emptiness. If a vase were not a vase, how could it be a pillar or anything else? You would have to say that the vase does not exist at all. If that were the case, since there would be no basis on which to explain emptiness, there would be no emptiness either. A perfect understanding of emptiness should reinforce your understanding of dependent arising. It should not deny the very existence of phenomena.

There are two types of illusion. One refers to emptiness, which means that although things exist, they do not have true or intrinsic existence. The other interpretation is that although they lack true existence, they project the appearance of existing in that way. When a magician conjures up an illusory horse, the magical horse appears to his visual perception. But in his mind he knows that it is deceptive and that it is not actually a horse. So he perceives its illusory nature. Similarly, when a person realizes emptiness, even when things appear to be truly existent, she sees them as illusory.

Until we reach a certain stage where we can really improve our understanding of emptiness, it is very difficult to discriminate between actual existence and intrinsic existence. Nevertheless, as far as existence is concerned, we need have no doubts, because it is testified to by our own experience. That is the premise on which we should apply the reasonings to negate the independent status or nature of phenomena, proving that they are dependent by nature. If you are able to negate that sense of independent existence on the basis of your own experience, then the mode of existence that remains will only be nominal, a mere designation or label. It is said that someone who has realized emptiness is able to discriminate between existence and independent existence. However, even that person is not able to explain it convincingly to someone else who has not realized it for himself or herself.

If we personally make an effort, the emptiness that we praise as the actual nature of the perfection of wisdom will initially be realized only intellectually. This realization is not the actual opponent force that can eliminate disturbing emotions. However, later, through constant familiarity with it, this realization can become the seed for bringing about the experience of clear light. That is the actual opponent eliminating disturbing emotions and inner delusion. But it needs to be supported by complementary reinforcing factors, such as the practice of compassion and the conventional awakening mind. The conventional awakening mind is the method aspect of the practice. Realization of emptiness, which is the ultimate awakening mind, is the wisdom aspect. On the basis of the union of these two awakening minds, it is possible to engage in the path that leads to the resultant state of a fully awakened being, the union of body and mind.

VERSES FOR TRAINING
THE MIND

*This is the work written by Geshe
Che-ka-wa as a result of his long experience
of putting the mind training teaching*

into practice. Known as the "Seven Point Mind Training," it forms the basis of this book, and I have quoted it throughout. Here it is in its entirety:

SEVEN POINT MIND TRAINING

Homage to great compassion.
The essence of this nectar of secret instruction
Is transmitted from the master from Sumatra.

You should understand the significance of this
    instruction
As like a diamond, the sun, and a medicinal tree.
This time of the five degenerations will then be
    transformed
Into the path to the fully awakened state.

I.

Explaining the preliminaries as a basis for the practice

First, train in the preliminaries.

2a.

The actual practice, training in the conventional awakening mind

Banish the one to blame for everything.
Meditate on the great kindness of all sentient
    beings.

Practice a combination of giving and taking.
Giving and taking should be practiced alternately
And you should begin by taking from yourself.
These two should be made to ride on the breath.
Concerning the three objects, three poisons, and
    three virtues,
The instruction to be followed, in brief,
Is to take these words to heart in all activities.

3.

Transforming adverse circumstances into the path to enlightenment

When the environment and its inhabitants
    overflow with unwholesomeness,
Transform adverse circumstances into the path
    to enlightenment.

Reflect immediately at every opportunity.
The supreme method is accompanied by the four
    practices.

4.
The integrated practice of a single lifetime

Train in the five powers.
The five powers themselves are the Great Vehicle's
Precept on the transference of consciousness.
Cultivate these paths of practice.

5.
The measure of having trained the mind

Integrate all the teachings into one thought.
Primary importance should be given to the two
    witnesses.
Constantly cultivate only a joyful mind.
The measure of a trained mind is that it has
    turned back.
There are five great marks of a trained mind.
The trained (mind) retains control even when
    distracted.

6.
The commitments of mind training

Always train in the three general points.
Engage vigorously in forceful means to cultivate
    qualities and abandon disturbing emotions.

Subjugate all the reasons (for selfishness).
Train consistently to deal with difficult situations.
Don't rely on other conditions.

Transform your attitude, but maintain your
    natural behavior.
Don't speak of others' faults,
Don't concern yourself with others' business.
Give up every hope of reward.
Avoid poisonous food.
Don't maintain misplaced loyalty.
Don't make malicious banter.
Don't lie in ambush.
Don't strike at the heart.
Don't place the load of a horse on a pony.
Don't sprint to win the race.
Don't turn gods into devils.
Don't seek others' misery as a means to happiness.

7.
The precepts of mind training

Every yoga should be performed as one.
There are two activities to be done at the
    beginning and end.
Train first in the easier practices.
Whichever occurs be patient with both.
Guard both at the cost of your life.
Train in the three difficulties.
Transform everything into the Great Vehicle path.
Value an encompassing and far-reaching practice.

Seek for the three principal conditions.
Purify the coarser ones first.
Practice that which is more effective.
Don't let three factors weaken.
Never be parted from the three possessions.
If you relapse, meditate on it as the antidote.
Engage in the principal practices right now.
In the future, always put on armor.
Don't apply a wrong understanding.
Don't be sporadic.
Practice unflinchingly.
Be liberated by examination and analysis.
Don't be boastful.
Don't be short-tempered.
Don't make a short-lived attempt.
Don't expect gratitude.

2b.
Training in the ultimate awakening mind

When stability has been attained, impart the secret
    teaching:
Consider all phenomena as like dreams,
Examine the nature of unborn awareness.
The remedy itself is released in its own place,
Place the essence of the path on the nature of the
    basis of all.

In between meditation sessions, be like a conjuror,
    a creator of illusions.

This is the short piece written by Geshe Lang-ri Tang-pa (1054–1123) known as the "Eight Verses for Training the Mind." This was the work that inspired Geshe Che-ka-wa (1101–1175) to go in search of a living holder of the mind training tradition. These verses were first explained to me when I was a small boy in Lhasa, and I have recited them every day since then as part of my personal practice.

EIGHT VERSES FOR TRAINING THE MIND

With the determination to accomplish
The highest welfare of all sentient beings,
Who surpass even a wish-granting jewel,
I will learn to hold them supremely dear.

Whenever I associate with others I will learn
To think of myself as the lowest amongst all
And respectfully hold others to be supreme
From the very depths of my heart.

In all actions I will learn to search into my mind
And as soon as a disturbing emotion arises
Endangering myself and others
I will firmly face and avert it.

I will learn to cherish ill-natured beings
And those oppressed by strong misdeeds and
    sufferings

As if I had found a precious
Treasure difficult to find.

When others out of envy treat me badly
With abuse, slander, and the like
I will learn to take all loss
And offer the victory to them.

When the one whom I have benefited with great
  hope
Hurts me very badly without reason,
I will learn to view that person
As an excellent spiritual guide.

In short, I will learn to offer to everyone without
  exception
All help and happiness directly and indirectly
And respectfully take upon myself
All harm and suffering of my mothers.

I will learn to keep all those practices
Undefiled by the stains of the eight worldly
  concerns
And by understanding all phenomena as like
  illusions
Be released from the bondage of attachment.